To God Be The Glory

Our Victories in Africa

Margaret Lovick

Acknowledgements

Special thanks to my God for letting me live long enough (88 yrs. old) to write this book. My husband, Bill Lovick, who went on to his reward on May 16, 1996.

Also, I thank my family and my children, namely my son William David Lovick and my daughter Marsha Ann Woolley and her husband Douglas Woolley. To my two grandsons Isaac Barry and Dimitri Woolley and to Rev. and Mrs. David Moore, the editors. I would like to thank our secretaries Rosemarie and Aria Zubler.

I am a living miracle and I thank God for his greatness and blessings in my life and in the lives of others that He touches through our ministry. All the honor and the glory goes to the Father, Son, and the Holy Spirit.

Introduction

From Genesis to Revelation, God's Word literally screams at us to remember, remember, and remember. When I would tell about experiences we had in Africa, people would say "please tell us more." So God began to deal with me. He told me to write it down. In fact, He said "write a book." So I trust this book will stir your heart. If you are a Christian, I hope it will cause you to remember the deliverance and miracles God did for you. If you are not a Christian, I trust you will accept Jesus as Lord of your life. Just say "Jesus, come into my heart. Forgive me of my sins. I believe you died for me. I accept you as my Lord and Savior." He will come into your heart and make you His child. Then begin to trust Him. He'll fight your battles and you will be surprised at the wonderful things he has in store for you. "For He is the same yesterday, today, and forever" (Hebrew 13:8). Moses said to the people to remember the day in which you came out of Egypt-out of the house of bondage-for by the strength of God's hand, the Lord brought you out. Guard these memories. Keep them fresh in your hearts. You are to remember what God did for you in the past.

Do you have a problem in your home, in your work, or in your family? The only way to face a giant is to do what David did: Remember the lion and the bear. David could only face Goliath without fear by remembering God's faithfulness to him when he killed the lion and the bear. I kept my father's sheep, and there came a lion and a bear who stole a lamb out of the flock. I slew both the lion and the bear and this uncircumcised Philistine shall be as one of them (1 Sam. 17:34-36). I am sure this is what David testified to Saul. David knew the danger he was facing, but he remembered his past and he looked Goliath in the face and said, "The Lord that delivered me out of the paw of the lion and the bear, He will deliver me out of the hand of this Philistine" (1 Sam. 17:37). You might say that was luck. No, I would say it was God guiding that stone. I would say it was a miracle. I can see Goliath standing with all his armor on, but God knew exactly where that stone would land. Hallelujah. So keep telling your deliverance and miracles to your children. It will build your faith every time you tell it, and it will build their faith. Why do you think there is not much faith in the world today? Because we have failed to remember the deliverances and miracles God has brought us through. Remember—don't let your generation forget. To God be the Glory!

TABLE OF CONTENTS

Chapter One

The noonday sun baked down on the steel-gray Peugeot as it rattled south along the dirt roadway leading out of Dahomey. Countless potholes riddled the desolate highway that cut through vast rolling grasslands spotted with trees. The driver, Bill Lovick, was a missionary. He was accustomed to West Africa's hazardous road system and kept the sedan moving at a steady clip of almost 40 mph. Only hours into the 800-mile trek that would take him and his family back to Lome, in the neighboring country of Togo (then known as French Togoland), Bill's thoughts wandered back to the conference he had just attended in Natitingou, where he had enjoyed the fellowship of several local pastors for a time of prayer, teaching, and strategic planning. He had a renewed sense of hope that the Gospel was getting a foothold in this region and would continue to strengthen as able native ministers, like those with whom he had spent the last few days, embraced evangelism. All in all, the conference had been a success, despite the dire warnings he had received about attending.

Only days before leaving for Dahomey, one of Bill's associates approached him with great concern:

Pastor I know you need to go to the conference in Natitingou, but please don't go. I had a dream, and I heard today that all the priests of the Ewe nation have met, and they are making juju. They have taken a nine-year-old girl and driven a thirty centimeter spike through her head. They removed her heart, brains, and liver. They have made fetish of her and have given her body to the fish gods. Please, Pastor, don't go!

No stranger to the brutal superstitious practices of this tribe, Bill knew that bad juju indicated misfortune was ahead. With reserved confidence he stated, "If God will keep us here, He will keep us there."

Still, more troubling words awaited him and his family when they reached their destination in Dahomey. Some of the local ministers attending the conference had received a revelation that seemed to confirm the earlier fears of Bill's associate. Speaking to those assembled, the ministers warned, "Your pastor and his whole family are going to die unless you fast and pray and win the victory." The conference attendees, like the church in Acts, prayed to God without ceasing. Several hours later, they sensed a release and a note of victory. The conference moved forward unhindered, and the Lovicks remained, unharmed. Calamity, it seemed, had been averted for now.

Clouds of reddish-brown dust trailed the Peugeot as it continued on its journey to Lome. The road was elevated now to accommodate the changing terrain. Each side sloped ten to fifteen feet down to meet an inhospitable muddle of rocks, dense grass, and trees. Bill glanced to his right to see his four-year-old daughter, Marsha, nestled safely next to her mother and peering out the open window at what through a little girl's eyes looked like the Grand Canyon below. Bill's wife, Margaret, was looking out, too, with an uneasiness that would surely pass once the road again leveled with the rest of the landscape.

Suddenly a loud boom reverberated through the frame of the car, jolting the family. The steering wheel began to pull to one side then the other as Bill realized that not one, but both of his front tires had blown. Trying to compensate for the sudden loss of control, Bill instinctively jerked the wheel while slamming the break pedal. His efforts proved disastrous as the car veered to the right and began skidding over the embankment. Margaret turned to shield her daughter, anticipating the inevitable impact of the car plunging into the rocks below. She shouted, "God, don't let us turn over!" No sooner had the words left her mouth when the car slammed into a tree, abruptly halting the fall. The impact collapsed the front end of the sedan, driving the steering wheel into Bill's chest and showering the family with hundreds of shards of glass from the shattered windshield. All three Lovicks were knocked unconscious.

Within seconds, Bill revived to find the front of the vehicle engulfed in flames and himself pinned and immobile. A man of stalwart frame and commanding presence, this former college football star seldom allowed any obstacle to restrain him. All of his efforts were fruitless, however, against the eighteen-inch ring of plastic and steel pressing against his torso. In desperation he cried out, "God this is not Your will! This is not what You said! You said we would build Your church, and the gates of hell would not prevail against us!" Marsha, who had now regained consciousness, saw her father struggling and the flames approaching. With dazed resignation she moaned, "We're going to burn to death." At that moment, a miracle occurred. Bill recounted, "I saw the hands of God come and bend that steering wheel out of my chest." Quickly the missionary slid out of the car and extinguished the electrical fire. He then turned his attention to his wife and daughter.

Margaret, ashen and still unconscious, was covered with blood. The dashboard and frame had sliced under her right arm, and the buckle of her seat belt had punctured her liver. Her husband, in agony from his splintered chest bones, struggled to remove his shirt and began wrapping his wife's wounds. Marsha, overcome with grief, sobbed, "Mommy is dead! Mommy is dead!" Bill, fighting back his own fears, stammered, "No...she's just unconscious." He eased Margaret from the crushed vehicle and seated her on the road, leaning her back against the door. He and Marsha began to pray.

Slowly Margaret opened her eyes. When she tried to speak, blood oozed out the sides of her mouth.

"How—is—it?" she asked her husband.

"It's bad," Bill replied, choking back tears.

The couple prayed and then Bill fetched the jug of water to quench his wife's thirst. After drinking, Margaret removed the scarf from her head, moistened it, and dabbed her daughter's forehead, which had been cut in the accident. As Bill turned to place the empty water jug back in the car, his wife suddenly lifted her hands and began speaking loudly in a strange language. Although Bill spoke five different languages at that time, he had never before heard the words rolling effortlessly off of his wife's tongue. He had a sense, though, that she was glorifying God. To his eye, her body was lifting from the ground, and he thought God was taking her. He cried, "God, please don't take her and leave me!" Margaret's body slumped to the ground as she slipped into a coma. Overwhelmed, Bill knelt beside his wife and began to weep.

Within minutes, the bush came alive with the rustling of grass and the whispers of approaching natives. They were Dendies, a godless tribe of mostly farmers and fishermen who had a history of cannibalism. Bill reached into the car to get his gun under the seat, but the Spirit of God checked him, saying, "Put it back. You don't need it. I have been here before you." The missionary stood amazed as a Dendi man with a bicycle and several women came out of the tall grass, "not with bows and arrows and spears, but with cruses of water and mats."

Marsha remembers the tenderness of the women as they laid her on a mat and washed her wounds. The man persisted in trying to communicate with Margaret and looked bewildered when he received no response. Bill asked him what he wanted. The man did not speak English but knew some French, and he replied,

A few moments ago all of us…heard a woman. She spoke to us [in our language], and she said you were servants of the Most High God, and God was with you, and He wanted us to take care of you and get you help. If we failed, God said He would strike us. We have come now, and the woman does not speak.

The man's words encouraged the missionary, who now realized that his wife's spontaneous outburst was God's direct summon for help. Desperately wanting to get medical attention for his family, Bill asked if there was a mission nearby. The Dendi man responded that there was a Serving in Mission (SIM) station only a few miles away; he would ride his bicycle to get help. Bill jotted a note and handed it to the man with instructions to give it to someone at the mission station. He watched the native, much older than himself, pedaling down the pocked highway, and probably wondered if he would ever see him again. He never did.

What seemed like an eternity passed before the faint but unmistakable sound of an approaching motor vehicle reached the ears of the stranded party. It was a pickup truck from the SIM station, and inside was a nurse and a missionary. The Dendi messenger had been true to his word. The SIM workers placed the Lovicks in the bed of the makeshift ambulance and headed back to the mission station.

The West African sun was now at its peak, adding to the discomfort of the exposed, parched, and aching travelers. Halfway to the SIM station, the truck sputtered and quit as it ran out of fuel. The SIM missionary went to get more gas, leaving the Lovicks and the nurse with the vehicle. Bill remembered, "By that time the pain and agony of broken and crushed bones hit all of us." Marsha, who was reclining in the front seat, began to cry, "Daddy, why did God forsake us? If God would give me a drop of water, I would praise Him all the days of my life." Soon the SIM missionary returned with gasoline for the truck and fresh water for the passengers. Seeing the water, an elated Marsha shouted, "Daddy, God cares! God cares!"

After arriving at the mission station, the driver and nurse carried Margaret in on the stretcher and set her on a bed. They provided another bed for Bill and a cot for Marsha. Before resting, Bill contacted Ted Shultz, a pilot friend, and apprised him of the need to get his family to a hospital as soon as possible. Ted replied that he was grounded because of the harmattan haze, a fog-like condition caused by the dust-laden West African trade winds. He would try the next day if conditions improved.

The pilot found a window of opportunity the following day, and he took it. The small plane provided by Speed the Light—a youth missions ministry of the Assemblies of God—could only accommodate Margaret and Marsha. Ted would have to return later for Bill. The plane lifted its broken human cargo and headed on a southeast course to the port city of Cotonou, Dahomey. There, missionary friends of the Lovicks were waiting to rush the patients to a nearby French military hospital. Before Ted could return for Bill, the harmattan haze blew in again, grounding the pilot until the next day. Although in tremendous pain, Bill took comfort in knowing his family was safe and receiving the care they needed.

When the missionary finally arrived at the hospital, he was stunned to see Margaret lying in a hammock suspended over a blood-soaked bed, her skin black from internal bleeding. The doctor's report painted a bleak picture: over three hundred lacerations, a broken ankle, broken ribs, a punctured liver, and over one hundred fractures in her hips from a femur that had been driven more than a foot out of location. The doctor said, "Pastor, your wife is not going to make it. There is no way she can live."

Hope seeped out of Bill with each somber word from the doctor. His wife was dying, and his four-year-old was suffering from a broken leg and broken ribs. His own condition, though not life threatening, left him little reserve to resist the barrage of dark thoughts pounding his mind. X-rays revealed that Bill had over eighty-one broken bones, necessitating an upper body cast from his neck to his waist. His range of motion now limited, he placed himself in a chair between his wife and daughter and tried to sleep.

News of the accident reached friends in the United States, and calls began coming in to the Lovicks. A pastor from Texas, E.M.

Yates, phoned and said, "Bill come home. We will pay your way." Phil Hogan, the executive director of the foreign missions department of the Assemblies of God, said, "Come home, Bill. Forget about Africa." In fact, there was nothing more that Bill Lovick wanted now than to see his wife recover, to take his family home, and to put Africa behind him. He had had enough of this adventure.

Margaret had been in and out of consciousness since the accident, and her condition continued to deteriorate. Her husband pleaded with the physician, Dr. Nkagoo, to do everything within his power to help his wife. The French-trained African doctor showed great empathy toward the missionary but knew that, short of a miracle, Margaret would soon die.

At one point while Bill sat looking at his wife, he noticed her eyes flutter, then open as she regained consciousness. Once again she struggled to ask how her condition was. Bill did not hold back.

"It is bad," he replied. "We are going home. We are going to forget all about this. We are going home."

"Did you ask God? Is that what God told you to do?" Margaret asked, puzzled.

"What have I to say to God!" Bill snapped, incredulous. "It is all over. We are no good to God. We are no good to anybody."

Realizing her husband had reached a breaking point, Margaret summoned her remaining energy to buoy his faith and remind him of the promise they had made to each other:

Remember when we were married in Orlando, Florida, and we gave ourselves to one another? Kneeling at the altar we sang, "Together with Jesus, life's path we'll trod, as one heart united by His hand we're led." We said we will never do anything with our lives without asking God. Bill, it's too late to change now. Take my hand.

Bill recalled later,

She pushed her hand that was bruised and torn and grabbed my fingers. She said, "Take Marsha's hand." I stood between those two beds, and I poured out my soul and heart like you would pour out a jug...I poured it all out before God. When I shut up, I heard an audible voice that said, "I'm God. I was with you, and I am with you. Stand still, and you shall see the salvation of your God."

Bill opened his eyes to find Margaret comatose. Her color was the same; her bones were still broken; and her vital signs remained unstable. But Bill had a promise from God, and he would cling to it tenaciously during the ebb and flow of choking thoughts of fear. He sat down next to the bed, exhausted, and gazed out the window at the rain that had begun falling. His wife's words were ringing in his ears: "Remember when we were married..." As Bill's mind drifted back in time, he recalled how God's hand had been on them even as children in Norfolk, Virginia, and had brought them together as a ministry team with a vision to impact Africa. He remembered how much simpler it was to follow God when they were young and carefree. And he allowed his thoughts to take him back to that time. A strange but comforting peace settled over him as he momentarily left the pain of the present and reminisced about the past they shared.

Chapter Two

During the early years of the Great Depression, Norfolk, Virginia was one of the few places in America still prospering. Nestled in the Hampton Roads area of the Commonwealth, just off Chesapeake Bay, it had become home to a growing number of navy bluejackets and their families with the establishment of a major US naval base during World War I. Millions of federal dollars flowed into the city as ships were modernized, barracks were erected, and piers were constructed throughout the 1920s and early 1930s.[1]

For Colonel E. Linwood Dew, Norfolk was the ideal location for his career and his family. He was stationed at Fort Monroe, which was about a dozen miles north of the naval base and served as armament headquarters for the US Army. Originally a seaman with the British navy, Dew had returned to America following World War I and steadily climbed the ranks in the US military. He oversaw the inspection of ships docked in Hampton, Virginia as well as in Charleston, South Carolina. A handsome man with chiseled features, blond hair, and blue eyes, Colonel Dew carried himself with a quiet self-assurance that gave the perception of aloofness. He had never been a religious man, had never conveyed an interest in spiritual things. He was a simple man who loved the military, and who loved his family. But as his wife, Ann, knew all too well, the military often took precedence.

Annie Hunter McCleary Dew was the perfect complement to her husband and seemed well-suited to being the wife of an officer. A striking woman, tall and full-figured with brown eyes and black hair that caressed the oval lines of her face, she had the look of one who was well bred. In contrast to her husband's British-style reserve, Ann, whose lineage was Scottish, was gregarious, fun loving, and sweet natured. But, as those who crossed her would attest, she had the capacity to show her ire if provoked. She also had the capacity to believe. Although originally not a disciple of any formal religion, Ann exhibited a spiritual hunger that eventually impacted her entire family.

Linwood and Ann had met during the First World War and were married on June 20, 1920. On March 2, 1922, there first child was born, a daughter named Margaret. Eighteen months later, Ann gave birth to a son, Hubert, whom Margaret affectionately called "Bubber."

By 1930, home for the Dew family was 1792 Fountainbleau Crescent, a comfortable colonial in the Lafayette area of Norfolk. Some of Margaret's fondest childhood memories occurred there: Sitting at her mother's feet, listening to her sing and talk about Jesus while she ironed clothes; playing church with Bubber in the backyard while other neighborhood children joined as willing congregants in the outdoor cathedral. It was a time of innocence, shaped by a mother whose presence and influence were always felt. "Mother never let us out of her sight," Margaret remembers. "She always knew where we were and what we were doing." And if what they were doing met Ann's disapproval, she was not afraid to play the role of disciplinarian. Margaret chuckles as she remembers the times that she and Bubber would run around the dining room table to avoid the dreaded razor strap.

Church attendance was not optional for the Dew children. Ann desired to provide a rich spiritual heritage for her offspring, and she made sure that Margaret and Bubber were in Sunday school every week, even though, ironically, she seldom attended any formal services herself. That would begin to change with the arrival of an evangelist from South Carolina who is remembered simply as Brother Turner.

Brother Turner was a traveling minister who held tent meetings throughout the South that were remarkable for their miraculous demonstrations. Margaret, who was eight years old the summer Turner arrived in Norfolk, was impressed with what she saw:

My mother and my Aunt Bell took my brother, me, and my cousins. We loved to sing the songs and listen to the messages, but the best part was to see all kinds of miracles right before our eyes. We saw the lame walk and the blind see, the deaf and dumb healed, and all kinds of miracles. In fact my aunt took my cousin up for prayer. She had seizures all of her life, and God healed her. She never had another one.

The experience strengthened Ann Dew's faith and brought added focus to her quest for God. Her church attendance, though still infrequent, showed more regularity. At home, Ann fully embraced her responsibility as a spiritual leader. She would read the Bible to her children regularly and pray for them tirelessly. Healing became a way of life for the family. Margaret recalls, "Mother always prayed for us. I never remember going to the doctor as a child—only for shots for school. We grew up with most of the childhood diseases like all kids, but no doctor was called, and we had no real problems."

In 1933, another revivalist rolled into Norfolk and reaped the harvest that Brother Turner had planted in almost the exact location three years earlier. Jackie Burris was a Baptist evangelist who preached a strong message of salvation. Entire families were moved to repentance in these meetings, including the Dews. Linwood, Ann, Margaret, and Bubber all went forward to surrender their lives to Jesus during one of the evening services. Later, they declared their conversions publically through water baptism.

Another family that was eternally impacted in these meetings was the Lovicks. They were originally from Greenville, North Carolina, and the road that brought them to Norfolk was paved with heartache and disappointment.

Robert Lee Lovick had worked as a carpenter on a tobacco plantation in Greenville that belonged to the father of Francis Marie Stevenson. The farm was bestowed on the Stevenson family's French ancestors for their military service during the American Revolutionary War. Robert was a handsome man and caught the eye of Francis at a country dance in 1924. Although fully aware that an illiterate tradesman was well beneath the social standing of her family, Francis married Robert without the consent of her father. It was a decision she would regret for the rest of her life.

Within four years, Francis had given birth to two sons—Robert Lee, Jr. and William Earl—and the marriage had deteriorated to the point of separation. Robert was a womanizer who showed little desire to change his ways. Divorce was unacceptable, so Francis moved with her boys to Norfolk to seek employment and a new life. She found her niche selling real estate and was eventually able to buy a home for her family at 6000 Gramby Street, which was about two miles from the Dews. Robert eventually rejoined Francis in Norfolk, but by the time Jackie Burris arrived, the marriage was still floundering, and the family was anxious for a fresh start. Like the Dew family, the Lovicks responded to Jackie Burris's altar call and committed their lives to Christ. Young Bill Lovick remembered that day as the happiest of his childhood.[2]

The Dews and the Lovicks, still unacquainted with one another, became part of a core group of believers from Norfolk Gospel Tabernacle that formed Glad Tidings Church the same year of the

Burris revival. In 1935, the church hired Arthur Graves as its senior pastor, and it began to grow spiritually and numerically.[3] Graves was no novice concerning the things of God. His father was F.A. Graves, a noted songwriter and evangelist who served as an elder in John Alexander Dowie's Christian Catholic Church in Zion, Illinois.[4] Elder Graves had spent years with Dowie and had seen both the miraculous touch of God and the excessive manipulations of man. He no doubt counseled his son to embrace the former and resist the latter because Arthur showed himself to be a pillar in the Church. Margaret remembers her pastor as a "wonderful teacher of the Word" and one who was "anointed and lived the Christian life before his congregation."

Under the leadership of Pastor Graves, Glad Tidings Church served as a spiritual incubator, providing a caring and protective environment that nurtured and encouraged more than a few to pursue the call of God on their lives. Graves established a foundation of prayer and evangelism at Glad Tidings. His early morning prayer meetings sometimes lasted as long as three hours.[5] His heart for missions was evident almost from the start when he stood before his new congregation and admonished them, "We have lost our vision for the lost, so I have decided that we give the first Sunday morning offering of every month to missions." God blessed this decision. According to Margaret, "In a few years we were able to burn the church mortgage and support many more missionaries around the world."

Margaret became very involved with missions at Glad Tidings, taking on the role of missionary secretary. She was responsible for

27

handling all correspondence with the missionaries supported by the church and, consequently, knew more about the needs of those in the field than the senior pastor. Pastor Graves observed Margaret's passion for her work and had her communicate missionary updates to the congregation periodically. On one particular Sunday morning when Margaret was speaking to the church, an unusual boldness came over her, and she began to preach to the audience about their responsibility to support those who were taking the Gospel across the globe. She concluded, "We were called to help send them, and God has called us to be faithful!" After stepping down from the platform, a woman approached Margaret and said, "I saw a vision while you were preaching. I saw a black man standing beside you, and he had a hood on his head. When he took it off, there stood Jesus." Unsure of what the vision meant, Margaret pondered it and opened her heart to whatever God had planned. Little did she know that His plan was to take her half way around the world with a young man she would marry from Glad Tidings Church.

Bill Lovick had hardly received even a passing glance from Margaret Dew for the first dozen years his family attended Glad Tidings, and there was no indication that the two would have a future together. Bill was six years younger than Margaret. While she was blossoming into a young, attractive Christian lady, he was still a boy. While she came from a stable, comfortable home, he came from a home of turbulence where fending off poverty was the only economic certainty known throughout much of his early childhood.

While Margaret embraced her mother's example of a virtuous woman, Bill shunned the self-absorbed, immoral model of manhood portrayed by his father. He saw a much loftier image of courage, faithfulness, and industry in his mother. And it was her example, more than any other, that prepared him for his life's work.

Francis Lovick was a tiny woman with a sharp mind and an indomitable will. Both attributes served her well in the aftermath of her most misguided life decision—marrying the carpenter from Greenville. Determined to provide for her sons when she separated from her husband, Francis went door to door, selling everything from silverware to encyclopedias to real estate. It was through selling real estate that she was eventually able to pull herself and her children out of poverty and into a position of respect in her community and in her church. Francis went on to become a multi-million dollar producer, exhibiting business acumen rarely found in the women of her day. Her tenacity to succeed in business was only matched by her desire to provide her sons a God-centered upbringing filled with her love and support.

Francis adored her sons. Even with her long hours of work, she always found time to attend their ball games and concerts. She made sure they were in church regularly, and she consistently prayed for God's will to be accomplished in their lives. Francis did her best to be a living example of a long-suffering believer. Long after she realized her husband was not only unfaithful but a polygamist (Robert had married another woman and fathered additional children while still married to Francis), she initially refused to divorce him or to speak badly about him in front of her sons. When she spoke about Robert Lovick, which was seldom, she referred to him only as "that man." When later in life she was asked by an inquisitive granddaughter why she never talked about "grandfather," she replied, "That man and I have nothing in common except for the fact that we have two of the most beautiful boys in the world. I would never say anything derogatory about him because they are a part of him, and I would never want them to think less of themselves. If you can't say something good about someone, you just don't say anything at all."

By the time Bill Lovick had reached his senior year at Granby High School in Norfolk, he had developed into a strong, confident young man who was popular among his peers. He had learned to be self-sufficient, teaching himself to drive on a Model A Ford and working odd jobs to pay for his school clothing.[6] He had shown great prowess not only on the football field but in the music room. Bill had won many honors as an opera singer and was once judged as Virginia's best tenor by opera great Lawrence Melchior. The University of North Carolina took note of Bill's abilities and offered him a full scholarship in the spring of 1948. The future was looking bright for the young man from Norfolk.

Perhaps nothing indicates the level of confidence Bill Lovick had achieved by the summer of 1948 more than the attention he gave to Margaret Dew. Margaret remembers, "Bill was always sitting on the back bench when I left church, and he would wink at me." Eventually the two began talking and before the summer was over, Bill took Margaret on what could be considered their first date, dinner at a quaint local restaurant. The two were fast becoming friends, but neither envisioned the relationship moving beyond that. Bill would soon be leaving for North Carolina and Margaret had charted a course to Florida with her brother to attend a new Bible college where Pastor Graves had recently assumed the role of president.

South-Eastern Bible Institute originated in New Brockton, Alabama, in 1935 as a ministry training center for men and women in the southeastern part of the country. In 1940, it temporarily merged with Beulah Heights Bible School in Atlanta, Georgia, and in 1946, the Board of Directors voted to secure a permanent location for the school in Lakeland, Florida.[7] In 1947, Arthur Graves was hired to establish the fledgling school in its new home, which he did with characteristic fervor. Many of the youth from Glad Tidings Church who felt a call to the ministry followed their former pastor to Florida, excited to be a part of this new adventure in God.

As the summer of 1948 came to a close, several of the youth from Glad Tidings gathered for one more evening together, enjoying each other's company before setting off on their chosen paths. Margaret and Bubber Dew had felt God drawing them into missionary work. The new school under Pastor Graves seemed the ideal place for preparation, and both were eager to go. Their mother, Ann, could not have been more pleased. Bill and Robert Lovick were both headed for the University of North Carolina, and though their father was delighted, their mother had her concerns. Margaret remembers Francis pulling her aside that night and saying, "Pray for Bill. I think he is going to the wrong college. He has a call to the ministry on his life." Whether Bill had shown any inclination toward ministry at this time is not known, but Margaret assured his mother that she would pray for him. And if there was one thing Margaret had learned during her years at Glad Tidings, it was how to touch heaven through prayer.

The youth group of Glad Tidings, under the strong, endearing leadership of Ruby Hart, focused much on prayer and on living a life that was pleasing to God. The group would meet every Sunday before the main evening service and inevitably spend time praying together. Quite often the presence of God was so tangible that the group would miss the service in the main sanctuary because they were on their faces before God in the youth hall. The glory and majesty of God had become very real to this close knit group of young men and women, and they were always hungry for more. And for Margaret, that hunger led her into the experience of being baptized in the Holy Spirit.

Ruby Hart's daughter, Mary, was one of Margaret's best friends. As friends often do when they experience something worthy of sharing, she began pestering Margaret to receive the baptism in the Holy Spirit. Margaret remembers, "This really bugged me. As I would go to the altar and seek [the baptism in the Holy Spirit, Mary and her friends] would hit me on the back and say, 'Hallelujah!' over and over again. It only distracted me." Margaret believed the experience was for her. Jesus had promised it in the book of Acts (1:8): "But you shall receive power when the Holy Spirit has come upon you; and you shall be witnesses to Me in Jerusalem, and in all Judea and Samaria, and to the end of the earth." The first disciples experienced it later in the same book (Acts 2): "And they were all filled with the Holy Spirit and began to speak with other tongues as the Spirit gave them utterance." The apostle Peter affirmed that the gift was for "as many as the Lord our God will call."[8] Margaret was sure that if she could just get alone with God, she would receive. And it was while she was praying for a stranger that God honored her faith.

Because Glad Tidings was close to the naval base, many service men would visit the church when their ships were in port. A young man named Harry Crittiten, on his way to the Pacific theater during World War II, attended a youth service and asked that those present would remember to pray for his safety. Margaret took his request to heart. That night, on her knees in her bedroom, Margaret had an encounter with God.

I began to pray for Harry that God would baptize him with the Holy Spirit, and I went on to tell the Lord how badly he needed it. Suddenly I said, "Thank you, Lord; I am next." I began to speak in a language I did not understand. As I was speaking, I saw this big bell going back and forth, gonging, and I [repeatedly] heard these words: "You are not your own; you were purchased with my blood." To this day I have never forgotten that experience. A few weeks later, we received a letter from Harry telling us that he had a chance to attend a church service in California, and there God baptized him in the Holy Spirit. Harry [eventually] returned from the war safely.

Once situated at South-Eastern Bible Institute, Margaret was assigned the responsibility of being the school's bookkeeper. She had worked for several years at a Norfolk bank following high school and was well qualified for her new position. Her office was located right next to President Graves, and she frequently saw Mrs. Graves, who was very involved in assisting her husband with the school's operations. One day, less than two months after Margaret had started at the institute, Mrs. Graves stopped by and announced, "I have a surprise! Guess what; Bill Lovick is coming to South-Eastern!" Margaret's mind immediately raced back to something that had happened a week earlier, and she began to conceive that God had used her to help Bill make his decision.

Since Francis Lovick's request, Margaret had prayed for Bill regularly. And recently she had been awakened at three o'clock in the morning with an unusually strong burden to pray. She woke her roommate, Katie Willets, and asked her to join her in the prayer room. For the next hour, the two women prayed in an unknown language, under the guidance of the Holy Spirit. For whom they were praying, they did not know, but when the burden lifted, they felt the need was met, and they returned to bed. "If I pray in an unknown tongue my spirit prayeth but my understanding is unfruitful. Sometimes we will never know when we pray in the spirit just what we are praying for, so if you are ever burdened to pray, please obey God " (1 Cor. 14:14).

Unknown to Margaret at the time, almost seven hundred miles away in Chapel Hill, North Carolina, Bill Lovick was awakened from a sound sleep. It was four o'clock in the morning, and God was speaking to his heart so distinctly that it almost seemed audible. He later related, "God told me I was in the wrong college [and said,] 'I have called you into the ministry.'" He then saw a vision of Margaret praying for him.

Bill called his mother later that morning to tell her of his unusual experience and his need to go to Bible college to prepare for the ministry. Relieved, Francis gave her blessing and said she would cover the tuition. When Bill's father found out about his decision, he was furious and said he would disown him. Undaunted, Bill withdrew from the University of North Carolina and headed south for Florida.

When Bill arrived at South-Eastern Bible Institute, he was wearing a bright red shirt and a sheepish grin. He sauntered up to Margaret and asserted, "Well, here I am," as if he assumed Margaret had been waiting for him since they said their goodbyes in Norfolk. Margaret shook her head and smiled. They renewed their friendship from the summer, and within months their relationship had deepened significantly. On March 2, 1949, while viewing the soft golden hue of a Florida sunset, Bill turned to Margaret and asked, "Will you be my life long girlfriend?" Margaret thought about it and replied, "I will have to ask my mother and dad."[9]

The courtship lasted just over two years. During that period, Linwood Dew retired from the military, and he and Ann moved to Orlando, Florida. Margaret had to leave school for health reasons and moved in with her parents, taking a job at a local bank once she recovered. Bill would visit her every weekend when he could. The weekends he wasn't with her family, he was traveling throughout the Southeast, singing with a quartette from the school. It was also during this time that he began developing his skills as a preacher. By the time he graduated in 1951, he had invitations to speak at churches throughout Alabama and Florida. It seemed as if he had found his calling as an evangelist.

On a sultry summer Sunday, on August 26, 1951, William Lovick and Margaret Dew exchanged marriage vows in a small Orlando church and embarked on a lifetime journey of serving God as a couple. After a brief honeymoon in Cypress Gardens, Florida, the two began traveling together throughout much of the Southeast and parts of Texas, spreading the Gospel of Jesus Christ.

In the meantime her brother graduated from Southeastern Bible College in Lakeland, Florida, and was married to Dorothy Lawrence a beautiful girl who was the daughter of Pastor and Mrs. David Lawrence. Hubert and Dorothy pastored in North Carolina for seven years. Then God called them to the mission field. Off they went to Grenoble, France to study French.

After studying French they arrived in the city of Ouagadou in Upper Volta, West Africa. Then the mission board wanted them to study the African language "More`." They studied under Rev. John Hall, a great man of God. After three months of study, God impressed Hubert with a special message which he wrote in English and translated it into More`. The title of his message was: BOM NI WATO TO." In English, it is "Jesus is Coming Soon." He addressed the Upper Volta Conference. He preached in More` with a heavy anointing, bringing tears to the eyes of the missionaries and the national pastors, stirring them all. The pastors were so stirred that they took the message back to their congregations. Then he gave an altar call which the missionaries said they did not do. This was quite an accomplishment, as this had never been done with just three months of study. After language study they went to their mission station in Kaya, Upper Volta. Hubert and Dorothy and Linny, their five year old son, went to their new home in Africa. Linny quickly made friends with the children, especially the gardeners little boy. This little boy was given to the gardener, because his family did not want him since he was crippled. Linny felt great compassion for him, so he stayed at the mission. During nap time, usually after lunch, Linny would go get him extra food and bring him some of his clothing. They became fast friends, and Linny would teach him about Jesus. The little boy received Jesus as his Savior and many days they would play church out under the mango trees.

Everything was going great in Africa. They were busy building churches and seeing souls saved. Suddenly Dorothy was taken sick. She was taken to a doctor in Ghana, West Africa, and he said she had to return home for surgery, as she was too sick to have surgery in Africa. Then Dorothy and Linny were sent home to North Carolina to Dorothy's mom and dad so they could get help. Dorothy wasn't getting any better, so when he received a telegram that she needed him, so he went home in 1960.

Well, Hubert and Dorothy were not allowed to return to the field, because of Dorothy's health. When they left the field there were twelve new churches under construction. There were 383 souls saved, who had stayed true to God and did not return to their witchcraft. This was in the Circle of Kaya. Because of their faithfulness and hard work in Berkina, Faso-the new name given to Upper Volta-there is a new 5,000 seat auditorium there, even to this day. To God be the Glory!

Within a few years, Bill began to sense God was calling them to the mission field. And it was in Terra Haute, Indiana, a few weeks before Christmas in 1954, that he began getting clear direction from the Lord that the mission field He was calling them to was Africa. When he shared this news with his wife, she responded dryly, "Have a nice trip."

Africa was probably the last place Margaret Lovick wanted to live. The thought of being so far away from her family was over-whelming. Images of cannibalistic tribes targeting her for their next meal left her blood chilled. She knew nothing about the country or its people. Even her friends advised against going. And yet the more she and Bill talked about it, the more something stirred inside of her. She knew they had to obey God.

The Lovicks placed themselves under the umbrella of the Assemblies of God Missions Department and began travelling from church to church to raise funds for their monthly support and for any equipment they would need. The culmination of their efforts came when they drove a station wagon down the aisle of the church building on the campgrounds of the Alabama District in Montgomery, Alabama. Margaret recalls, "We stood amazed and watched our precious people fill the wagon with money to buy the things that were needed. The people of Alabama were very faithful to God. Every church we visited wanted to have a piece of equipment on the mission field."

Their funds secured, all that was left for the Lovicks was to pack their belongings and say their goodbyes. "Packing to leave for Africa was an extensive undertaking," Margaret remembers. "Barrels had to be packed with food and clothing to last for three years. Boxes had to be built for our bed and equipment. [Everything] was shipped to New York and stored in an Assemblies of God Foreign Missions [warehouse] until notified to be shipped to Africa."

Bill and Margaret visited her parents in Orlando to bid them farewell, knowing that they would not see them again for several years, if ever. "We were told by the Missions Department that we could not come home even if there was a death in the family," Margaret recalls.

Bill's mother, brother and his brother's family drove the couple to New York harbor where the steamship M.V. Italia was docked and waiting. On Friday morning, July 15, 1955, after a tearful goodbye, the Lovicks crossed the gangway and boarded the ship. The lonesome droning of the ship's horn as the vessel pulled away from dock signaled to the untried missionaries their departure from a land of abundance and familiarity and the beginning of their journey into the heart of darkness and the vast unknown.

[1] Norfolk: Historic Southern Port by Thomas J. Wertenbaker Page 329-330

[2] Grandfather Remembers: Memories for My Grandchild by Bill Lovick. Page 21

[3] Glad Tidings Church History. Accessed June 2, 2008 http://www.gtcag.com/site/dbpage.asp?page_id=140002195&sec_id=140002095

[4] The Historic Legacy of Zion's Christian Assembly. Accessed June 2, 2008. Page 5 http://christianassemblyzion.org/images/History.pdf

[5] Glad Tidings Church History. Accessed June 2, 2008 http://www.gtcag.com/site/dbpage.asp?page_id=140002195&sec_id=140002095

[6] Grandfather Remembers: Memories for My Grandchild by Bill Lovick. Page 20, 22

[7] Southeastern University website. Accessed June 26, 2008 http://catalog.seuniversity.edu/content.php?catoid=6&navoid=81

[8] The Holy Bible NKJV. Thomas Nelson Publishers, 1988. Acts 1:8, 2:4, 39.

[9] Grandfather Remembers: Memories for My Grandchild by Bill Lovick. Page 25

Chapter Three

Almost a week after leaving New York, the M.V. Italia docked in La Havre, France. A missionary, named Kenneth Ware, met Bill and Margaret at the pier and drove them to Paris. Since the Lovicks were being commissioned to serve in a French-speaking African nation, it was imperative that they become steeped in the language before reaching their mission field. Paris would have been the ideal city for this training, but the cost of living was beyond what the young couple could afford. Geneva, Switzerland was the better choice. So after spending one night in the "City of Lights," Bill and Margaret boarded a train and headed almost three-hundred miles toward the Alps.

Switzerland is a pluralistic European country that recognizes four different languages as the official languages of the nation. In Geneva, which borders on France, French is the primary tongue. The Lovicks arrived at the city's central train station and quickly realized that the region's dialect was not the only cultural challenge they would be facing. Bill instructed Margaret to stay with the bags while he paid a visit to the restroom. He returned rather quickly with a look of shock on his face. He told his wife, "You wouldn't believe it! I thought I was in the wrong place. A *lady* came in and sat a few rows down [from me] and said, 'Bon jour monsieur.'" Their training in diversity had begun.

The studio apartment that became home while the Lovicks were in Switzerland could hardly have been better. Only a few years old, it contained a small kitchen with a refrigerator, a private bathroom, and comfortable furnishings—the one exception being the sofa bed that was stuffed with coarse straw. The apartment was owned by a local sheep herder named Pierre, whose sister, Margaretti, befriended the Lovicks and introduced them to her church. Margaret remembers, "We had a wonderful time of fellowship with the Christians, and they were so good to us. Every Sunday [they] took us to their home or to a restaurant for a good meal. The people were so kind, and they all greeted us with a kiss on both cheeks. This, we found out, was the custom, which was very nice. We felt wanted."

Once settled, the couple began their French studies in earnest, sometimes feeling discouraged at their slow progress. As any new student of a foreign language can attest, slight mispronunciations can sometimes have embarrassing results. For Bill, who was practicing his French on this local church, this occurred during one of his Sunday morning sermons. Preaching passionately on his subject, "The Eyes of God," Bill slurred the French word "*yeux*" so that it sounded like "*oeufs*." What the congregation heard was an anointed discourse on the "eggs" of God, rather than the "eyes" of God.

After eight months of immersion in the French language, Bill was walking through one of the local markets and heard a woman ordering a kilo of *pommes de terre* (potatoes). It dawned on him that he clearly understood everything the woman was saying. When he returned home to Margaret that day, he informed her that they were ready to go to Africa.

Although their time in Switzerland was brief, the Lovicks had established a cherished bond with the local believers. At times when missionary funds were delayed, the local Christians sent provisions to the Lovicks to hold them over. Even as the missionaries prepared to leave, Margaret remembers, "They loaded us down with gifts, especially chocolate candy." After a tearful farewell, the missionaries boarded the plane that would take them first to Paris and then to the land that had been tugging at their hearts — Africa.

The contrast between Switzerland and Africa could not have been greater for Bill and Margaret Lovick. Leaving the majestic, snow-covered Alps, they descended into a barren desert landscape spotted with thatched roof huts that looked like ant hills from the sky. They escaped a harsh European winter with record-breaking cold only to melt in the oppressive tropical climate of an unseasonably warm West African March. Even the reception they received when they arrived at the mission compound in Ouagadougou, Upper Volta, was a stark contrast from the sendoff they received in Switzerland. Margaret recounts:

> We saw a big banner over the front of the building saying "WELCOME." We were told that it was not for us, but that it was for someone who had arrived last week. Then we were fed a meal and told this was the last free meal we would receive. They charged us for all of the meals.

Living quarters for the missionary couple was a long garage equipped with a wash basin and a shower and furnished with a bulky iron bed covered with a mosquito net. The bed rested on wheels, which proved quite useful on the nights when the air inside was stifling and the only relief was to roll the bed outside under the stars. Bill and Margaret spent their first night in Africa sleeping under the "canopy of heaven," only to be awakened by an early morning storm that quickly covered their bed with sand and rain. Still visible on top of the mosquito net were snake skins, remnants of a nocturnal visit from some venomous serpents, and a reminder to the missionaries that their survival, more than ever, would depend on an uncompromising trust in God and an informed awareness of their new surroundings.

Not long after their arrival in Ouagadougou, the Lovicks received word that the shipment of the supplies they had stored in New York arrived at the port city of Accra, Ghana, about 700 miles away. They hitched a ride with another missionary couple who needed to go to

Tamale, Ghana to cash their monthly support check. Once in Tamale, Bill rented a truck and later drove to Accra for the supplies. During the layover in Tamale, while the missionaries were counting their money in the compound where they were staying, Margaret spotted something unusual outside the window: "I saw a man behind the truck without a stitch of clothes on, and he had greased his body so that you could not hold him if you caught him. He was glistening in the moonlight." As it turned out, he was waiting with his partner for an opportunity to rob the missionaries. Margaret recalls, "Bill saw [them], got his shotgun, and ran out on the porch and shot up in the air. I was right behind him with a baseball bat." The two thieves fled naked and empty-handed into the night. Before long Bill would have a chance to use his gun again, but the results, then, would be lethal.

Back in Ouagadougou, the Lovicks settled their belongings into a mud building that was used as an infirmary during World War II. There had been a problem with wildcats roaming the compound during the night, so Bill was on the lookout for them and was prepared to shoot them once they were spotted. One evening he heard what sounded like animals fighting in the yard, and he grabbed his shotgun and went outside. Seeing two eyes peering from a tree, Bill took aim and fired, thinking he was shooting one of the wildcats. What dropped dead from the branch was a shimmering white Angora cat that belonged to a missionary couple in the compound. And the owners were not easily consoled. A dark cloud of mourning hung over the compound for days, leaving the Lovicks feeling all the more alienated in their new home. They decided to leave for a short time and visit a nearby Bible school, where they had the opportunity to teach while the tumult from the shooting accident subsided.

While away, the Lovicks received a telegram inviting them to attend the annual mission conference in Natitingou, Dahomey, in the latter part of 1956. The couple accepted the invitation, which turned out to be another God-ordained moment. While there, the Lovicks were selected to join another couple as missionaries to Bassari in Togo. This obscure West African village would become the place where God laid the foundation for the ministry He had planned for Bill and Margaret Lovick.

Located in north-central Togo, Bassari sits in the midst of a major cotton growing area at the base of the Togo Mountains and is populated primarily by the indigenous group that is the village's namesake. In the late 1950s, the Bassari people lived in circular stone huts with cone-shaped roofs usually covered with thatch[1]. Family ties were strong in this village, and the homes were clustered in units that corresponded with those family connections. Amidst the network of stone and thatch dwellings sat the mission station founded by David and Claudia Wakefield, the missionaries to whom the Lovicks were sent to assist.

The Wakefields and their four children left an indelible impression on the Lovicks. "They really sacrificed to build the [mission] station," Margaret remembers. "We helped and worked together like a hand in a glove. We prayed for one another and shared like ministers should do. They taught us what missions is all about."

The two couples accomplished much in a short span of time. Within months, they completed building the first Christian church in Bassari and dedicated it to the Lord. Not long after that, the missionaries launched a technical school where students learned to be carpenters and mechanics. The village provided ample opportunities for them to ply their new found skills. Margaret recalls, "When trucks came through the village and broke down, the students were able to repair them. [The students were also taught to] put metal roofs on churches and [other] buildings and to make tables and chairs and beds."

Claudia Wakefield and Margaret kept busy teaching the village children in Sunday school. On occasion, they also visited the compound of the local chief to help his many wives and to bring them the Gospel message. Margaret recalls, "The women and girls were not allowed to go to school. They were to be slaves and wait on the men and bear children." Margaret taught the women and girls what she knew of French and, more importantly, what she knew about sanitation.

The water quality in Bassari was very poor. Impurities in drinking water abounded. Margaret taught the women of the village a simple process for filtering their drinking water through tightly woven cloth so that they would not contract the dreaded Guinea worm disease. Larvae from the Guinea worm, once ingested, can burrow into a human intestine and develop into a three foot worm that slithers its way to the lower limbs of the infected individual, causing swelling joints and burning blisters as it attempts to exit through the skin. Once the worm begins its exit, which can take weeks to complete, the only thing the patient can do, according to Margaret, is to "take a little twig and wrap it around the worm and roll it a little each day until it comes out." Margaret's filtering technique was a welcome blessing to the village women and their families.

As is often the case for missionaries, periodic furloughs are required to replenish funds and get much needed rest from their labors. The Wakefields had been laboring almost nonstop before the Lovicks arrived, and now assured that their work was in good hands, they left for the United States to reconnect with family and to raise additional funds, so the work in Africa could continue to move forward.

The Lovicks had proven themselves more than capable of managing the mission station, but Bill was struggling with the language of the region. Although French was the official language of Togo, and Bill had become adept at communicating in that tongue, everyday conversation for the people of Bassari was in Kabiye, a language peculiar to northern Togo. When he went to the village to minister, Bill would preach in French, and his listeners would look at him with puzzled expressions. He would return to the mission station discouraged but determined that he would master the local dialect. Bill made a vow to the Lord that he would learn the Bassari language at the rate of 25 words a day. As with his experience learning French, the day came when he felt confident that he could deliver a sermon in Kabiye. He returned to the marketplace and stood before the people to preach. He tried his best to say, "Jesus loves you. God loves you," but the villagers just shook their heads and said, "We don't understand what you are saying." The problem was that there was no word for love in their native dialect. Bill returned to the mission station, got on his face before God, and prayed, "Dear God, unless you help me, I will leave and never come back. My heart burns with zeal to help these people."

One night, sometime after praying this prayer, the missionary had fallen asleep outside reading his Bible. He awoke around 2:30 in the morning, lit his lantern, and began to read John 3:16, "For God so loved the world that He gave His only begotten Son." Bill prayed, "Help me to understand this Scripture in Bassari. Let me be able to tell these people Your message that You love them." He then remembered the words of a young Bassari mother whom he had heard express joy at giving birth to her son. In her native tongue she said, "My heart feels strong for this child, from the top of my head to where the dirt scratches my feet."[2] Bill grabbed a pen and paper and began to write, "For in the beginning God felt with His heart for man. God felt so strong in His heart for man that He gave His Son as a living sacrifice to redeem man from sin. That Son came and felt so strong in His heart for man that He gave His life." Bill felt confident that God was giving him a message that the Bassari people would understand.

Later that morning when he arose, he returned to the village to deliver the sermon he received from the Lord. When he finished, a man said, "We know what you mean; we know what you say." That day, Bill saw his first Bassari man give his life to Christ. Sobbing at Bill's feet, the man cried, "God in His heart feels for me!"

[1] **Togo**." Encyclopedia Britannica. 2009. Encyclopedia Britannica Online. 3May2009 <http://search.eb.com/eb/article-281768>.

[2] Pugh, Jeanne. "20 years in Africa were well worth it." St. Petersburg Times 11 Feb. 1978, Crossroads: 4D.

Chapter Four

Less than a year after arriving in Africa, and only months after arriving in Bassari to help the Wakefields, the Lovicks found that their ministry had, by the grace of God, advanced to a remarkable degree. In their February 1957 newsletter, the couple rejoiced in what God was doing:

We are happy to report to you from our work here that God is blessing and that the kingdom of God is advancing. In the past month many Africans from this area have denounced their heathen ways, laid down their burdens, taken up their cross and followed Jesus.

At the present time the mission house is almost completed. Our Sunday School and [day] school building is well underway. In our day school we have 91 students enrolled, in our Technical School 47 young men, and in our Bible School [we have] 31 young men preparing to preach the gospel. [...] we have 150 villages where the gospel is taken each week, and this year we are launching a new campaign to add another hundred villages to this great network.

Bill continued to preach the message that God had given him for the people of Bassari—that God in His heart loved them—as often as the Lord led him. And the message continued to change lives. Perhaps none was changed more dramatically than that of a leper who lived in the bush, a woman named Atsi.

Bill's encounter with Atsi began somewhat mysteriously in the village of Rolonca, just around the hill from Bassari. The missionary was preaching to a crowd that had gathered in the village when suddenly he saw a woman standing off a short distance in the midst of the bush, somewhat hidden by the tall grasses. He could see that she was a leper—her nose and lips had been disfigured by the disease—and that she looked old. As he continued to preach, Bill heard the voice of God speak to him on the inside, directing his attention to the outcast creature: "My son, I have brought you here to tell her that I, with My heart, feel for her." Bill responded by preaching the message God had given him, and when he gave an altar call, nineteen people accepted Christ as their Savior. But the old woman did not come. When Bill searched for her after the meeting, she was nowhere to be found. He asked the villagers if they knew where the old leper woman was, and they replied, "We did not see her."

"She was right here in the bush," Bill explained.

"There is no one here like that," they said.

Bill went home puzzled, with a burden in his heart for the woman in the bush. "My heart and soul would not let me rest. I saw that woman in my mind. I saw her in my heart. I could not rest because of her. I prayed, 'God just give me one more occasion to tell her of Your love, Your mercy—to tell her that You love her and feel for her.'"

Three weeks passed, and there was no sign of the old leper woman. Then one Sunday morning as Bill looked out the back door of his church, he spotted her, broken and naked and staggering toward the church building. He watched as she teetered down the church aisle on two round balls of emaciated flesh that once were feet, leaving a wet, irregular trail of rotting tissue as she continued past the seats filled with people, found an empty chair, and sat down. Instantly those around her left their seats and stood along the wall to escape the stench and decay. Bill had planned on preaching from the Book of Psalms that morning, but God said, "No, tell them once again that I, with My heart, feel for them, that I love them."

Once again the missionary declared the message of God's love, and once again he gave an invitation for people to come forward and accept Christ. The old leper woman struggled to her feet, and for the first time, Bill saw the woman's hands. "On her left hand there were no fingers at all, just a thumb. On the right hand there was one finger and a thumb." She almost fell as she came forward and stood at the altar. Her eyes pierced those of the missionary as if probing to find deceit. She said, "White man, white man. Do you lie to me?"

Bill answered, "No mother, I lie not to you."

The leper, relaxing her shoulders slightly, said, "Never in my life has anyone felt in their heart for me."

Bill responded, "But old woman, your father, your mother, with their hearts they felt for you."

Her shoulders drooping further, she replied, "No—no—never." After a slight pause, she began to tell her horrid story.

When I was a child of five or six years old, my father saw the blotches, the pimples, and the white. I came to my father. He said, "Atsi, close your eyes. Daddy is going to play a game. Tell Daddy where he touches you." He took a piece of Kapok cotton and he touched my ear. I said, "You are touching my ear." He touched my neck. I said, "You touched my neck." He touched my nose and my lips. I said, "You are not touching me Daddy, you are only playing." Then my father took his knife and said to me, "Close your eyes. Daddy is going to play a serious game with you." He cut the end of my nose open, and I didn't feel it. He cut my lip open, and I didn't feel it. I said, "Daddy, you are only playing." But suddenly blood began to drip. I looked and said, "Daddy, what have you done?" He said, "Atsi, you are a leper. The law of the Bassari people is that no leper can live in the village. He is condemned to the

forest—condemned to die, to perish among the wild animals."
I pleaded with my father. He said, "Atsi, I can do nothing.
The law is the law."

The old woman told of how she was brought before the elders
of the village and condemned as a leper. The men of the village took
her to the mountains and left her, screaming, to die alone. The law
was the law.

Atsi learned to live by a new law—the law of the bush. She spent
her first night in a tree, clinging for safety from the leopard or the lion
that might have caught her scent of fear and found her to be easy prey.
She eventually made her way further up the mountains and lived in
the tombs amongst the baboons. Years went by, and she survived on
roots, leaves, berries, bark, ants, worms, anything that was edible. A
total recluse, she saw people only from a distance. She said,

Several years after I had been in the forest I wanted to see.
My eyes became hungry to eat of the face of my mother and
father. I came and pushed the bush away. The men saw me,
but they didn't come and help me. They sicked their dogs on
me—the Basenjis, hunting dogs of Africa. These dogs that
don't bark ran after me. A pack of them knocked me down
and ripped and tore until I was lacerated from head to foot.
Then the men came up and kicked me. They said, "You are

not wanted. Never come back. Next time we will let the dogs eat you. Don't ever come back again."

The old woman continued her narrative, telling how she went to the high priest of the Bassari nation and begged him for help. He would help on the condition that she become his slave. Young Atsi, who by then had seen the leprosy spread to most of her body, accepted his offer. While serving as slave to the high priest, she helped him sacrifice eleven children. "I participated in the eating of their flesh and the drinking of their blood," she said. Her teeth, filed to jagged points, attested to her cannibalistic practices.

Having emptied herself of her gruesome tale, she looked up at the missionary, her shoulders still drooping, and asked, "Can God with His heart feel for me?"

Bill responded, "Atsi, the Lord came not for those who were whole, but the Lord came for those who were sick and needed a physician. That is you, Atsi."

The old woman, looking for an idol or charm that she could feel or see, asked, "Where is he? Is he in your home? Is he in your car? Where is he? Where do you keep this Jesus?"

Bill replied, "God lives in us."

Atsi, lifting her head and shoulders, raised her voice in accusation, "Oh, oh you were lying to me. You have lied to me."

"No, no," Bill reiterated, "God lives in us."

Bill watched as Atsi absorbed his statement. Then he explained to her how she could find Jesus and ask Him into her heart. He invited her to kneel at the altar and pray. The old leper woman struggled to her knees. Bill remembers,

Her hands slid across the altar rail leaving a trail of filth from leper hands. I knelt across from her. The odor was like I [nothing] I had [ever] smelled in my life. But I prayed [silently], "Dear God, You love this woman. You have died for her. Help me dear God to love her enough to tell her of Your love and Your mercy." I called [to] the people of the church, and I asked them to come and pray for her. We began to pray, and I have never felt the power of darkness so strong. It was like an iron ceiling that pressed down upon our heads. We could not break through it. It was total darkness. I told the people to keep on praying. I took four of the men, and we went into the prayer room and prayed. We sought God from the depths of our hearts. It must have been a half hour or more, but they were still praying in the auditorium when we came out. We laid our hands on that old woman, and [...] the Holy Spirit came upon us as we began to intercede by the power of Almighty God.

Bill felt something touch his arm; it was Atsi's leprous left hand. He started to draw back but resisted the urge and kept praying. Soon after, Atsi wept her way into a relationship with Jesus and said, "I know that God with His heart feels for me. For I, with my heart, feel for God."

The women of the church cleaned and dressed Atsi, who, after more than fifty years of living alone, once again had a family. Though on the outside her body still showed the deformities of a leper, on the inside her spirit blazed with a love for her newfound Savior and His people. From that point on, Atsi was the first to arrive at church, coming as early as 5:00 a.m. to pray before the service. Her commitment to the things of God was as one who loved much because she was forgiven much. And like the woman who brought Jesus an alabaster flask of fragrant oil, Atsi was determined to bring her own sweet-smelling offering to her new Master.

One Sunday morning, Bill announced from the pulpit, "Next Sunday is our harvest festival. We bring a harvest to God, the first fruits—our sheep, our goats, our chickens or guinea fowls, the fruit from our fields." Atsi heard this and said to the Lord, "Dear God I have nothing to give You." She left the church that day with a heavy heart, earnestly desiring to bring an offering to the Lord. But having no farm and no animals, she was unsure as to how she would honor God.

Whether she was led by the Holy Spirit or by her survivalist instincts is unsure, but Atsi struck on an idea to go to the village of Kolonga, over eleven miles away. She walked through the night on her stubbed appendages and arrived in the morning, determined to have an audience with the village chief.

She reached the chief's residence and was ushered into his presence, where she struggled to kneel. Tribal law stated that she should click her fingers twelve times when she came before the chief, but Atsi had no fingers to click. Protocol also required her to touch her nose to the ground, then lift her elbows above her head and thump them twelve times on the ground. This she did. The chief said, "Rise. What do you want?" Atsi replied with the innocence and simplicity of a child:

Chief, next Sunday in our church, everybody who loves God is going to give God a love offering. I love God. I feel for God in my heart, and I have nothing to give to God. I know you are digging peanuts in your fields. Can I go behind the men who are digging those nuts? Can I look into those holes before the baboons and monkeys get in there and find the stray nuts that I might have an offering to give to God?

The chief approved Atsi's request, and for the next four days she went to the peanut fields. When the men had finished digging up a row, she would follow and begin her work. Using her thumb and the nub that was once a finger, Atsi would reach into the holes to extract any remaining nuts, one nut at a time. By the third day her hands were so raw from digging that she had to resort to using her feet.

Placing her right foot into the hole first and getting her balance, Atsi then plunged her left foot in and moved it in circles around and up her right leg in a screwing motion to lift any stray nuts to the surface. When her left foot would start bleeding, she would switch to using her right foot until, finally, on the fourth day she had filled her basket. Atsi said to herself, "Now I have an offering to give to the Lord."

Harvest Sunday came, and Bill Lovick was standing in his pulpit. The congregation was singing, and some were beating drums as they brought their offerings to the Lord. Bill recalls,

The people began to pour down the aisles with their baskets of peanuts, yams, eggs, chickens, whatever they had, bringing it to God. I looked down the aisle of the church and coming through the back door was Atsi. In her arms she was carrying half a calabash that was just over the top with peanuts, bringing it to God. I looked at her feet. They were raw. I watched her come. She got almost to the altar. There was a little boy who was bringing a chicken to the altar. Instead of carrying that chicken, he was going to be different. He had a little stick, and he had that chicken tied to a string. He was going to make that chicken walk all the way to the altar. Just as [the boy] got even with Atsi, that chicken gave a jerk and broke that string. The little boy, not seeing [Atsi], took off after the chicken as fast as he could. He hit Atsi's elbow, and her peanuts went all over the floor.

Atsi stood there as if frozen in time and then began to weep freely. Before the rest of the congregation knew what had happened, many of them, while making their way to and from the altar, had stepped on and crushed the nuts that had fallen to the floor. Atsi cried, "Dear God, I wanted to give it to you. I wanted to give you an offering, but now, Lord, it's gone." Some of the women nearby heard her and immediately stopped the people from trampling on the nuts. They scooped the fragments from the floor and put them back into the calabash. One of the women lifted the calabash and was going to help Atsi by carrying it to the altar for her. Atsi shouted, "No! No! It's mine! Let me take it! Let me give it to the Lord." Bill remembers,

As [Atsi] came closer, I saw her hands. She had no skin on them. I saw her bring that offering and lay it on the altar. God spoke to me and said, 'Bill Lovick, never in your life have you seen an offering as great as this, and never in your life shall you see an offering like this one." But I said, "Dear God that is only four or five cents worth of peanuts." God spoke to me and said, "It is the giver." I said [to Atsi], "Atsi, God loves you. God in His heart feels for you." We all lifted our hands, and we praised and glorified God.

Atsi looked at her pastor and asked, "Does the Lord love me enough to heal me because I brought Him an offering?"

Bill replied, "Atsi, if you had nothing to bring to God, He loves you enough to heal you."

"Would you pray for me after the service?" Atsi asked.

"No, we will pray for you right now," Bill said, reaching for a bottle of peanut oil. He had never anointed anyone with oil before, but he knew it was scriptural, and he figured peanut oil was as good as any other type of oil. He pulled the stopper from the bottle and poured the oil on Atsi's head until it began to run down her body. The congregation joined him in asking God to heal her of her leprosy. For three consecutive Sundays, they repeated this ritual with no apparent change in Atsi's condition.

On the fourth Sunday, as evening service was about to begin, the congregation heard someone approaching the church, singing with all her heart, "He hath touched me, He hath touched me, God hath touched me." Atsi entered the building, walked up to the altar and said, "Pastor, the Lord has touched me."

"Tell me about it, Atsi," Bill said.

"No let me tell the whole congregation," Atsi insisted.

Atsi turned and faced the people and began to tell of how she was preparing her dinner in a big clay pot held over a fire. As she was mixing in water and meal, the pot slipped from her grasp. She dropped her spoon and tried to grab the pot before it fell. For the first time since she was a little girl, she felt a burning sensation. The heat from the pot had burned through her bandage and reached her skin.

And she felt it! The nerves that had been deadened by leprosy were being rejuvenated. Atsi continued her testimony,

I took the bandage off [my hand], and I reached up. I felt my ear. I felt it! I felt the rocks coming to church beneath my feet! Oh I never knew the church floor was so cold. When I came in and put my foot on the concrete, I didn't know it was so cold. The Lord is healing me!

Five weeks later, Atsi did not have one open leper spot on her body. She had been healed by the power of Almighty God.

From time to time, the church at Bassari hosted special services dedicated specifically to helping believers receive the baptism of the Holy Spirit. On one such occasion, Margaret was praying with Atsi, who was eager to have all that God offered her. That morning, fifty-seven people had received the Holy Spirit, and the sanctuary was filled with the joyful praises of the recipients. Margaret motioned to Bill to join her in praying with Atsi. Bill walked over, placed his hands on Atsi's head and said, "Dear God fill her with Your Holy Spirit." He remembers,

Suddenly Atsi began to drink in the blessings of God. That tongue began to articulate, and suddenly that tongue began to speak in a language Atsi had never [learned] in her life. A language she had never [learned] one word [of]. It happened to be the tongue I had heard from my birth. She began to speak in beautiful English, "The Lord is my Shepherd, I shall not want." And for over ten minutes she spoke in English under the anointing of the Holy Spirit as she was filled with the power of God.

Atsi became a great spokesperson for the Lord. She would venture out to wherever the Lord led her, leaving a half day early to walk to places others could get to in a fraction of the time. When her body finally gave out, and she went home to be with her Master, her church family remembered her as the greatest blessing that had ever come into their lives.

Chapter Five

In early 1960, the Lovicks returned to the United States on furlough to raise funds for their work in Africa. They did not know it at the time, but the Lord was preparing to expand their sphere of influence on the mission field, and it was going to require a vehicle that was capable of taking them over some rough terrain. The Lord had a remarkable plan for providing this vehicle, a plan that hinged on the obedience of one simple man. And his obedience ultimately touched hundreds of souls a continent away.

It all started at the close of a Sunday morning service in a small country church in Martinsburg, West Virginia. The pastor had given Bill the pulpit to tell the congregation what God was doing in Africa. When Bill finished sharing his message, he invited anyone present to come forward to accept Christ as their Lord and Savior. An old share cropper in bibbed overhauls slipped out of his pew and walked up to Bill. He said, "Your message touched my heart. I am not a Christian, but I want to give my life to Jesus Christ. [And] God spoke to my heart to give you my jeep. That jeep is all I own in this world, but God said, 'Give it to the missionary.'"

Bill replied, "I am not concerned about the jeep. I am concerned about you." The two men knelt down, and Bill led him in a prayer for salvation. The old farmer wept as he surrendered his impoverished, timeworn life to the Master. When the prayer was finished, the two men stood up, and the old man self-consciously wiped his wet cheeks with his sleeve. Bill placed his hand on the man's shoulder to reassure him that he understood what the man was feeling and that there was no need to feel ashamed. The man told him his name was Henry Moon, and he was serious about giving Bill his jeep. Bill recalls,

> He took me outside to see the jeep, which was well used. His wife heard him telling me to take the jeep, and she jumped all over him with both feet. I thought she would whip him right there. I tried to talk him out of it. I did not want to hurt his feelings, but I knew the jeep would not make it, for it was in too bad of condition. But [Henry] insisted that I take the jeep because God told him to give it to me.

The pastor of the church heard about Henry Moon giving Bill his jeep, and he became suspicious. He confronted Bill after the service and asked him if he had talked Henry into making the offer. Taken aback by the accusation, Bill responded, "I did not know he had a jeep. God spoke to him, and if you have any complaints, you register them with God." Seeing that the pastor was unmoved, Bill said, "I'll tell you what I will do. Monday morning, before he can get the title changed, I will be out of town." Somehow, Henry Moon got wind of Bill's plan and was back at the church at 5:30 that evening with his jeep. He said to Bill, "I have everything in order, the insurance included."

"Brother Moon, are you sure God wants you to do this?" Bill asked.

"Yes I'm sure," the farmer responded confidently.

Bill laid his hands on the jeep and dedicated it to God's service. Moved and humbled by the new convert's simplicity of faith and obedience, Bill then asked God's blessings on Henry. When he was through praying, Bill offered to drive his benefactor home, which was about fourteen miles from the church. Henry refused Bill's offer saying, "I don't want to take up any more of your time. God is going to take care of me." And the old farmer walked away.

Bill and Margaret drove the jeep from West Virginia to Bill's mother's home in Norfolk, praying for Henry Moon along the way. Shortly after their arrival, the Lovicks received a letter from a man named Howard Lindsay in Orlando, Florida, who wrote, "God told me you were taking an old jeep to Africa. God told me to tell you not to take that old jeep to Africa." Enclosed was a check for $345, which Lindsay said would cover the difference in cost between the old jeep and a new one. Bill told Margaret to send the check back to Mr. Lindsay because it would cost much more than that to upgrade to a new vehicle. Margaret refused, saying, "I am not going to send it back; God has a plan."

"You do what you want to," Bill replied.

Later that same day, Margaret asked her husband to take her shopping, saying, "Billy, get the jeep out, and we'll go in it." Bill remembers,

I got the jeep out, and we went down Granby Street and then down Sewells Point Road to Military Highway, where the naval base and Little Creek Road and the amphibious base all come together. Suddenly in the middle of that thoroughfare, my wife yelled out, "Woe!" and I stopped. I said, "Where is the oil tanker that is about to run over us?" The jeep stalled, and here all of the naval base traffic and all of the army base traffic, and all of the Little Creek traffic met [and began honking]. I had all of the traffic blocked, and no one could move until I moved.

Bill looked over to his wife and asked her why she told him to stop. She pointed across the road to a red jeep sitting on the lot of a car dealership. "Look over there on that lot," she said. "That is our jeep. God said it was ours for Africa." Just then they heard a siren; the police were coming to see who was blocking the intersection. Bill cranked the engine over and over, trying to get it restarted, but to no avail. In desperation he told Margaret to lay hands on the vehicle and pray, which she did, and it started. Bill pulled away just as the police car arrived, and he drove over to the lot where the red jeep was parked. Bill remembers, "It was a beautiful jeep—six cylinder engine, wrench on the front, oversized tires—just what we needed for Africa." He looked at his wife and said, "Margaret, they will want $5,000 for it."

"No, that is our jeep. We are going to take it home with us. Just be quiet."

"You are nuttier than a fruit cake," Bill responded.

"Just be quiet. That's our jeep," Margaret insisted as a salesman made his way toward the couple.

Bill got out of his car and introduced himself to the man and explained that they were missionaries and needed the jeep to take to Africa. The salesman explained that he could sell it to Bill at a good price because nobody was interested in buying a red jeep. This was the first time the manufacturer had offered the color red for this model, and apparently it had not been a big seller. For $1,450 plus the old jeep from Henry Moon, Bill and Margaret could drive the new jeep off the lot and take it to Africa. Bill countered by saying, "I will give you $345 and my jeep." The salesman just laughed. "But you don't understand," Bill said, "I want to take this jeep to Africa to go from village to village and tell [people] about Jesus."

"I don't care if you want to take it to heaven and take St. Peter from cloud to cloud. The price is $1,450," replied the salesman.

Bill walked back to his car and said to Margaret, "Let's go."

Margaret prayed as Bill climbed inside the old jeep. As he started the ignition, a truck pulled in, blocking his exit. Bill motioned for the driver to move, and the man, who was delivering a sign for the dealership, replied, "Mister, just wait a little bit, and I will be out of your way." Bill looked at the sign: H.H. Lurhing Motor Company. Immediately he wondered if this was the same Lurhing who was his old college roommate. Bill inquired of the salesman, who confirmed that the owner had a son who went to Bill's school and who was working at the dealership with his father. The salesman tried to locate Bill's old roommate, but he was out of the office at the moment. The salesman suggested that Bill take his wife shopping for an hour or so, and he would try to reach the younger Lurhing and ask him what kind of deal he could make for Bill on the jeep.

The Lovicks drove off the lot to a nearby store and bought some items for their return to Africa. When they left the store, Bill drove home a different way to avoid the car dealership.

"Why are you going this way?" Margaret asked her husband.

"I'm going this way because we can drive right to the boat tomorrow. See we are just about out of gas. [This way] we won't even have to buy a dollar's worth of gas."

"Billy, you go back by that dealership. We are going to drive that red jeep to Africa."

Bill reluctantly turned the car around and pulled up to the dealership and parked his old jeep along the road. "What are you parking here for?" Margaret asked.

"So when he says 'No' I can drive around that pickup and go right straight home," Bill responded.

Margaret glared at her husband: "You drive up and park beside the jeep, so when he says 'Yes' we can put our packages in the jeep. You can unscrew the license plate and put it on the red jeep."

Bill drove up and parked beside the new vehicle, and he noticed the salesman walking toward him shaking his head. Bill murmured to his wife, "He can't even wait to get here to say, 'No.'" When the salesman reached the Lovicks, he said to Bill, "Sir, I thought you were the craziest man I've ever met, but I met a man who is twice as crazy as you are. His name is Henry Lurhing. Mr. Lurhing said you can have the jeep for your $345 and your jeep, and he will pay for all the paperwork and the license transfer." Bill stuck his head in the door and looked at his wife. She said, "What have you got to say now?"

"I've got nothing to say but praise God!" Bill replied, smiling.

Bill loaded the packages into the new jeep, transferred the license plate, signed the papers, and drove away rejoicing with Margaret at God's extraordinary provision. In less than two months, the new red jeep was in Bassari, Africa, where God was about to unveil His manifold wisdom to the young missionaries. The red jeep that had escaped the notice of so many American consumers was being anticipated patiently by a begrimed and contemptible tribe deep in the bush lands of West Africa.

Shortly after returning to Africa, Bill felt the nudging of the Holy Spirit, leading him to minister to the Losso tribe. Knowing this tribe's reputation for being unsanitary ("They hang their meat up to cure, and when it gets bugs on it, they eat it."), Bill was reluctant to go. Once he was sure of the Lord's direction, he paid a visit to his African associate, Claude, and told him, "God said He wants *us* to go minister to the Losso tribe."

"He told *you* he wants *you* to go among the Lossos," Claude responded. "Well aurevoir, goodbye. God has not said one word to Claude, so I'm going nowhere where there are Lossos."

"Claude, come and go with me to the prayer room. Let's pray about it," Bill said, coaxing with his hand.

"No, I'm standing here flat footed telling you 'No.' You will get me in that prayer room, and I'll say 'Yes,' and I don't want to go." Within a few minutes, Claude began to cry and said, "Lord, I'll go where You want me to go, even among the Lossos."

Three days later, the two men packed the jeep and started out for Losso country. Roads were scarce in this region, but the jeep traversed effortlessly across the open country and bush lands. The travelers spent their first night along the Oti River, which flows Southwest through Togo and Ghana, emptying into Lake Volta. Claude took a bucket and went to the river to draw some water. When he returned, he was clearly shaken.

"Claude, what is wrong?" Bill asked.

Claude stuttered, "Mon...mon...mon, Pastor, I saw a snake bigger than a tree!"

Bill followed Claude back to the river where they found and killed the reptile—a water python that was over 33 feet long and 43 inches around. The two men skinned the snake, and Claude cooked and ate the tail for dinner. Bill showed less culinary daring and fixed sardines for his dinner that evening.

As darkness fell, the men stretched out in the jeep to get some sleep. Just as they started to doze, they heard the thundering roar of a lion, so close that, according to Bill, "it sounded like he was in our hip pocket." Claude, who was laying across the back seat, stammered, "Wha...wha...what was that?" Bill, in the front, tried to reassure Claude: "It was only a lion."

"Pastor, has this thing got a reverse in it?" Claude asked.

"Yeah," Bill responded.

"If we had any sense, we would put this thing in reverse and go back where we came from," Claude reasoned.

"Claude, go back to sleep," Bill admonished as he switched on the headlights, revealing the bushy mane of a nearly 500-pound lion directly in front of the vehicle. Bill started the engine, and the lion inched closer. He honked the horn, and the lion moved closer still. Claude, peeking over the seat, said, "Pastor, don't do anything else, or he will be in the jeep with us." Bill continued to honk the horn and flash the headlights, and the lion eventually turned around and walked off. The rest of the night, Claude was on edge whenever he heard a sound. "Did you hear that Pastor?" he repeated until Bill thought morning would never come.

At dawn, the trip resumed, and the men traveled until mid-afternoon when they approached the tributaries of the river. Five or six women near the river bank saw the red jeep and immediately started running and screaming, "Go rama hale tow! Go rama hale tow! Go rama hale tow!" Bill asked Claude, who was familiar with the native tongue, what the women were saying. He explained that what they said could be interpreted, "They just got here. It just got here. Everything just got here."

Perplexed, Bill asked, "What do they mean?"

"I don't know," Claude replied, "but I am praying to God they are not saying dinner just got here."

Bill said, "Claude, let's pray."

"If we haven't prayed before now," Claude responded, "we are in trouble."

The two ministers bowed their heads and prayed. Bill remembers that the Lord gave them the deepest peace they had ever experienced. In the minutes that followed, they would need every bit of it.

They began to drive further along the river when they heard the sounds of beating drums. They looked up and saw hundreds of Lassos lining both sides of the river, armed with bows and arrows and spears and shields. Out of this group stepped a wrinkled man about sixty-five or seventy years old, totally naked but for a monkey skin cape shading his head from the sun. He walked toward the missionaries' vehicle with a steady, purposeful gait, and His gray hair and beard gave him a look of venerability. As the man approached, Bill slowly opened the door of the jeep while easing his hand onto the Colt 45 strapped to his hip. Immediately the Lord checked him to put the gun away, so he loosened the holster and left it on the floorboard of the jeep, reaching, instead, for his Bible. Bill began to walk toward the old man, clutching his Bible. When the two men were about eight feet apart, the native suddenly stopped and asked Bill in the language of the Lossos, "Yovo, are you the one for whom we have been waiting for a long time?"

"For whom have you been waiting?" Bill asked as Claude interpreted.

"We have been waiting for one to come and open the heavens and show us the true and living God," the man replied. "Are you the one?"

"I have come," Bill answered.

The old man, not completely convinced, said, "Let me see..."

"What do you mean?" Bill asked.

"Four years ago...," the man started to explain, but then paused, looked aside, and called out, "Paga, paga! Come old woman; you are the vision. Come quickly!" An old woman came forward and stood before them, her head bowed in submission. The old man resumed his narrative, saying that the woman before them had seen a vision four years earlier of a black man and a white man coming across the tributary on a four-wheel bicycle. (This group of people had never set eyes on a car or truck, but they had seen a bicycle, so that was the only way they could describe the vehicle in the vision.) The white man in the vision held a key in his hand that would unlock the heavens and show the Lossos the face of the true and living God. The old man looked at Bill and asked again, "Are you the man?"

"I am that man," Bill replied.

"Let my eyes see," the man said, turning toward the jeep and squinting. "Bega, Bega!" he called. "Come quickly child, and bring me a kapok pod." A little boy raced off and returned swiftly with a seed pod from a nearby kapok tree, handed it to the old man, and then ran back up the hill. The old man took the seed pod in both hands, wrenched it, slammed it against a rock, and watched kapok seed scatter everywhere. He scanned the fallen debris intently and then reached down and seized a small bug—probably a cotton stainer, which is known to feed on kapok seeds. He walked over to the jeep, brushed off the dust on the fender, and set the bug on it. The man turned to his left and shouted, "Bang tong na wingo!" He turned to his right and shouted the same words again. The crowd that had gathered along the hill came alive at the man's words and began to shout in astonishment and delight. Bill asked the man what he had said. Pointing to the red bug sitting on the fender of the red jeep, the old man said, "Four years ago, the woman told us the color of your four-wheel bicycle was identical to the color of the kapok beetle. I have put my eye on him, and I cannot tell where one starts and the other stops."

Bill stood speechless as he contemplated the precision in God's unfolding plan and the number of people that the Spirit of God had been leading to get Claude and him to this exact place at this exact time. He was thrilled to know he was right in the middle of God's plan for that moment of his life.

The two missionaries followed the Lossos back to their huts and began unpacking the jeep. They were hungry and exhausted from the travel and excitement. The old man approached Bill and asked, "When are you going to let us see God?"

"But Papa, we are tired [and hungry]," Bill pleaded.

The man stood looking at Bill for a moment. Tears began to well in his eyes and run down his weathered and dusty cheeks as he said, "Is the hunger of your belly greater than the hunger of our souls that would see God? Is the desire to lay your body down greater than for us to lay the load that we have carried all our lives?"

"No," Bill responded.

As Claude continued to unpack, Bill grabbed a lantern and walked over to a weathered and polished log and sat down. The people gathered around and sat down to listen as dusk lowered itself upon the camp.

"[I] read the Gospel of John and translated it into Kotokoly, a language they could understand, until three o'clock in the morning," Bill remembers. Claude relieved Bill at that time and continued teaching the people until daybreak. The two missionaries rotated like this for five days and nights, expounding the Word of God. And the people stayed. And the people listened. At the end of the fifth day, Bill and Claude extended an invitation to the people to accept Christ as their Lord and Savior. Five hundred and nineteen souls came forward to surrender their lives to Jesus. Bill was astonished by the response and asked them if they understood what they were doing. In unison they replied, "We understand. We have waited a long time."

One by one, the new converts brought their heathen gods, doused them with kerosene, and threw them into a fire. All the while they rejoiced and sang with Bill and Claude about the wonder working power of the blood of Jesus. The spiritual fire that was kindled that night spread throughout the nation. And it was the simple obedience of a humble farmer from West Virginia who was led to give his old jeep to a man of God that opened the door for God to move.

While he was alive, Henry Moon never knew how much his simple act affected a generation half a world away. But he knew of God's faithfulness. Not long after giving his jeep to the Lovicks, Henry was visited by a man who owned eight car dealerships throughout the United States, and one of them just happened to be in Henry's town. While at the local barbershop, the visitor heard two men talking about a crazy man from their church who gave his jeep away to a missionary. The Chevrolet dealer, moved by the story, found out the name of the man and the name of the church he attended. After making a few calls, the businessman discovered Henry was a sharecropper and paid him a visit on the farm where he was working. The car dealer introduced himself and told Henry he had heard the story about the jeep. He said, "Your sacrifice touched my heart. I want to do something for you." He brought Henry to one of his dealerships and said, "I want you to go and pick out any pickup that you like, and it's yours. It's yours."

Years later, Bill was preaching in Clearwater, Florida, and a little old lady walked up to him following the service. Shaking Bill's hand, the woman said,

Pastor, I am Henry Moon's wife. Henry died two years ago. [After] he gave you that jeep and made that sacrifice, I could have left him because we had to bum rides until we were given a pickup truck. Pastor, from the day he obeyed God, everything he touched turned to gold. When he died, Henry left me plenty of money, a home paid for, and forty-five acres of land—more than I'll need for the rest of my life.

Bill thought about God's plan: *What if Henry had failed and Margaret had failed, and what if Mr. Lindsay and Claude and I had failed?* God laid it on the heart of someone to paint jeeps red. If anyone had failed, there would be a lost tribe that would never have heard of Christ's love for them. They would still be waiting and looking for a red jeep and a message of hope. But God's plan did not fail because those who played a role believed in the words of the song: "Only one life; it will soon be past. Only what is done for Christ will last."

Bill's faith was strengthened by what God had done through he and Claude and him in reaching the Lossos, and he decided to expand their sphere of influence by traveling south of Bassari to Bondague (Bongoulou?), which translated means the region of the damned. When Bill and Claude arrived in the village, the locals, mesmerized by the sight of a white man, gathered around the jeep to observe Bill. Seeing he had an inquisitive audience, Bill used the opportunity to tell them about God sending His Son to die for them and about Jesus rising from the dead. He told them that salvation was a free gift from God to them and showed them how they could receive that gift.

The chief of the people, who had been listening, confronted Bill and called him a liar. He said that he had never heard about such a God, so it could not be true. Bill responded to the chief's rebuke by telling him that it was not God's fault that the chief had never heard about this. The chief responded, "You are a liar! Go from us! If God loved us He would have sent someone to tell us. Go! You are a liar!"

Bill strongly believed that Christians are responsible for reaching the lost of their generation, regardless of their nationality or language and that God would hold them responsible for doing so. With this sense of responsibility and urgency, Bill lifted a prayer to God on behalf of the people of Bondague (Bongoulou?) as he and Claude began to leave: "Dear Lord, let us not fail You. Show us the way Lord!"

Walking toward the jeep, Bill spotted a man on the side of a nearby hill stretched between two logs, his hands and feet bound with rope. One of the locals told the missionaries that the man was at the mercy of the sun god, Wanaba, and that he had been tied there for three days. Bill and Claude walked over and knelt beside the nearly lifeless form, whose face and hands were stained with blood. Bill whispered to the man, "My friend, I have come to help you." The man did not respond. Bill and Claude began to pray, "Dear God, You love this man. You love his people. Jesus, somehow get hold of this man. You love him. You sent us for him. Jesus, help him now." A woman behind the missionaries shouted at Bill, "He failed! He failed! His god can do nothing!" Bill and Claude stood up and made their way toward the jeep while the sound of drums and chanting mounted in the background, echoing the woman's refrain: "He failed! He failed! His god failed!" The missionaries drove away weeping.

When they arrived at the mission station in Bassari, Bill immediately went to the church and banged on an old oxygen tank that was used as a bell to call the people. Once everyone was gathered, Bill told them the story of what happened in Bondague (Bongoulou?) and of how the townspeople resisted the Gospel message. One of the old men in attendance reflected, "They were just like we were before we heard God's word."

Bill asked the congregation to pray for the lost people of Bondague (Bongoulou?) and for the man tied to the logs. For three days and nights several Christians fasted and prayed. After the third night, they notified Bill, who had just returned from ministering in another village, that the burden had lifted, and they believed God had responded to their prayers. With that good news, Bill broke his fast, had some dinner, and went to bed.

In the pre-dawn hours of the next morning, Bill was awakened by the sound of someone clapping at the back of the house. He grabbed his flashlight, opened the door, and yelled, "Who is it?"

A voice replied in the stillness, "Do you know me? Do you know who I am?"

"I can't tell by your voice," Bill replied. Searching with his flashlight in the direction of the sound, he suddenly saw a long spear and a naked savage beside that spear.

"Do you remember me?" the native, named Jordien, asked. Immediately Bill remembered the man on the hillside tied between two logs. He swung open the door and said, "Yes, I know you! You are the man from Bondague (Bongoulou?)! Yes, I know you. How did you get here?" Jordien dropped his spear and told Bill his story.

I knew when you came. I knew when you called me "friend." I wanted to cry out, but I was not master of my mind or my voice. I had been condemned. I was to die. When you left, I wanted to cry out, "Help me! Don't leave!" but I could not. That night it rained. The next day the sun arose, and I became very hot. As I laid there, I prayed to Wanaba to let me die. Then suddenly, way down inside of me, way down, the words that you spoke, that you mentioned, [came back], and I began to say [to myself], "Jesus, Jesus, Jesus." My insides began to cry out, and I said that name over and over and over. Suddenly, like breaking through a great barrier, from my belly into my being and through my mouth came the words, "Jesus, Jesus, Jesus!" The people came. They said, "He is saying the name of the white man's god." They cut me loose from the logs and took me to the chief. I was still crying, "Jesus, Jesus, Jesus!" The chief said, "Take him home."

I asked my wife to forgive me for killing our baby, for I had bashed his head against a rock and drank his blood. She forgave me and gave me some food, and I rested. I asked someone to come with me to find you, but they would not come. So the next night I began my journey [through a forest filled with snakes, panthers, and lions] all alone with only a spear. But I did not fear, for every time my foot hit the ground, I would say, "Jesus, Jesus."

Having finished his story, Jordien fell to his knees before Bill, and grabbing his hands, pleaded, "I have walked all this way to ask you one question. Please tell me who or what is Jesus." Bill knelt beside Jordien and told him about the sacrifice at Calvary to redeem us from our sins. Jordien wept his way into an acceptance of Jesus Christ and was born into the kingdom of God. He stayed for some time at Claude's compound and attended church faithfully. Before he returned to Bondague (Bongoulou?), God filled him with His Holy Spirit. Within a few years time, over twelve churches were established in the region of Bondague (Bongoulou?), all because someone took the time to tell a condemned man about the saving love of Jesus Christ.

The years 1960 and 1961 were the worst of times and best of times for the Lovicks. Within months after returning to the field in late summer of 1960, after a short furlough to the United States, Margaret contracted dengue fever, a life-threatening disease that, like malaria, is transmitted to humans by mosquitoes. Also known as break-bone fever, dengue is accompanied by high fever, severe headaches, and tremendous muscle and joint pain, and Margaret seemed to be experiencing it all.

To keep his wife from dehydrating, Bill kept her covered with blankets soaked in well water. He also tried to keep her strength up with regular meals. But at the worst possible time—when his supplies were almost depleted—a heavy rainstorm washed out all the roads to Ghana, where the nearest supply stores were located. Bill found a bit of flour and salt and made Margaret a dry biscuit and some tea. He knelt down beside her bed to pray for her and asked her what she wanted for dinner that night. Unaware of the scarcity of supplies, Margaret said, "I would like some roast beef. I'm so hungry. And make lots of gravy." Bill thought she might as well have asked for the sun and the moon.

Reluctant to ask the Africans for provisions after he had told them that God would supply all of their needs, Bill got alone with God and began to worship. Bill recalls,

Suddenly I felt a hand slip into my right hand. It was so real. I thought Margaret had gotten out of bed, but when I looked up, no one was there. Then I realized it was God. I began to praise and worship Him fervently, when suddenly I heard a clap at the door. Without thinking, I pulled my hand away to answer the door. I looked everywhere, but I never found that hand again.

At the door stood a boy about fourteen years old who was as naked as the day he was born. He said to Bill, "Pastor, the postmaster sent me to tell you that there is a package at the post for you." Bill thanked him and wondered how he would pay for the package if postage was due; he didn't even have a penny to his name. When Bill arrived at the post office, the postmaster greeted him, wearing nothing but boots and a hat. (Bill always joked that the postmaster was the best dressed man in the village.) The man said, "Pastor, I don't understand this. There was no mail for the army or the commandant, no mail for the government, only this one package which weighs forty kilos (ninety pounds). I don't know what to charge you as there are no papers with it. So just take it."

Bill looked at the package and saw that it was from the Women's Missionary Group of Prichard, Alabama, which likely meant provisions of some sort. He praised God all the way home, laid the unopened box at the foot of Margaret's bed, and proceeded to cut away all of the wrapping paper. He reached inside of the box and pulled out a can of Libby's roast beef and gravy. It was as if God had personally taken Margaret's dinner request, weeks before she knew she wanted it, and then arranged to have it shipped to her and Bill. The missionaries were overjoyed at God's provision. In all, there were twelve cans of roast beef, twelve cans of corn beef, mayonnaise, jams, crackers, cookies, and a can of Crisco.

But there was more. At the bottom of the box was a 45 RPM record by the McGuire Sisters. Bill placed it on their record player and heard these words of encouragement:

If you believe, your worries will be few.
If you believe, your dreams will all come true.
Have faith in God. Remember, there is nothing God can't do.

Every time the song ended, Margaret asked Bill to play it again. After the sixth replay, the room was filled with the glory of God as the couple worshipped and praised Him. Suddenly, Margaret jumped out of bed and started dancing. God healed her instantly. And the fever never returned. The couple feasted on a dinner of roast beef and gravy and crackers that night, rejoicing in God's goodness. Later that evening, God spoke to Bill as he was reading his Bible: "I will be what I must become. What I have never been but what you need, I will become. I am for the glory of My church and for the glory of my people. Praise Me and worship Me and ask in My name anything; it is yours. You are mine. I am yours. Praise Me and worship Me, and I will come in your midst and be glorified."

In late fall of 1960, a man named Bower, one of the elders of the church in Bassari, came to Bill and said, "Pastor, I am praying that God will give you a crooked arm."

"Bower, please, I have enough trouble as it is. I don't need a crooked arm."

"But Pastor, you don't understand, I mean a crooked arm to carry a child."

"Okay, you keep praying then."

Shortly after that, Margaret experienced episodes of vomiting. She thought it was something she was eating. When it did not subside, Bill took her to visit an African doctor in the town of Sokode, almost 40 miles from Bassari. When that doctor had no answers, they traveled 125 miles west to an Indian doctor in Tamale, Ghana. He informed the couple that Margaret was pregnant. The two were elated. For Margaret, it was an answer to prayer—she had asked the Lord for at least one child. The doctor gave Margaret a variety of vitamins and asked her to return in six months. He determined that she would need to stay in

Ghana for the last three months of the pregnancy, so she would have access to adequate medical care.

When the time came to relocate temporarily to Tamale, Bill made arrangements with pilot Ted Schultz to transport Margaret by plane. Bill would travel in the jeep with their houseboy, Koffie, to bring all of their belongings. The people from Glad Tidings in Norfolk, Virginia, had shipped a full supply of gifts for the new baby, so Bill packed those in a foot locker along with Margaret's clothing and loaded them into the jeep the night before they were to leave.

That evening, heavy rains and a flash flood washed out the main road out of Bassari and the airfield behind the mission house where Ted was to pick up Margaret. Ted called Bill and said he was grounded in Sokode and was advised not to fly because of the fog and rain. He said a local missionary, Wayne Turner, would drive his truck as far as he could into Bassari. If Bill could drive his jeep to where the road was washed out, they could then walk Margaret to the truck, and Wayne would drive her back to Sokode. When the weather cleared, Ted would fly her to Tamale. The planned worked wonderfully.

Once Bill got word that Ted and Margaret were in flight, he started off with Koffie in the jeep. It rained all the way to Tamale. Often the bridges along the way were covered in water, so the two had to spread rocks across the bridge decking to gain traction. Because of the poor conditions, the normally six-hour trip took sixteen hours.

Margaret had the best of care in Tamale. Dr. Maajan, a Pakistani physician, had just come to Ghana from the United States where he served his internship at John Hopkins Hospital and the Mayo Clinic. He specialized in performing Caesarean sections. At one point during her stay in Tamale, Margaret started passing water but showed no signs of labor. Dr. Maajan examined her and decided to put her in the hospital where the baby could be monitored on the hour. After fifteen days, Dr. Maajan determined that delivery by Caesarean section would be best for Margaret and the baby.

On September 1, 1961, Margaret was taken to the main operating room on the ground floor of the hospital. The room had shuttered windows that let in outside light, so Bill stood outside one of the windows looking in and taking snapshots with his camera. He watched as they put Margaret on the operating table. A male nurse then began to administer general anesthesia by placing a cloth over Margaret's face and having her inhale gas. She immediately felt like she was drowning. Afraid that she might fall asleep and never wake up, Margaret threw the towel from her face. Dr. Maajan, seeing her anguish, came to her side and reassured her. Once Margaret was sedated, the doctor quickly performed the operation. Within minutes, Marsha Ann Lovick—a 7 lbs. 2oz. girl with blue eyes and black hair—made her entrance into this world. Her father could not have been happier. "The little girl is a doll. She is really a beauty," he wrote to family. "Everyone says she looks like me."

Margaret lost quite a bit of blood during the ordeal, and there wasn't enough of her blood type in the hospital's reserves. An announcement was made over the local radio station requesting blood donations for the American mother. An executive from the Proctor and Gamble

Corporation was in town and heard the radio announcement. He just happened to have Margaret's blood type and had his driver take him to the hospital where he donated blood for Margaret and left a money gift for baby Marsha.

Bill and Margaret were once again awed by God's provision for them. "Here we were in the bush of Africa," Margaret remembers, "and God sends one of the best surgeons all the way to Africa when He knew I would need help. Then He speaks to the heart of a stranger who came and gave blood. God is so good!"

Before the Lovicks could travel back to Togo, Bill had to go to the American consulate in Accra, the capital city of Ghana, and establish an official record of Marsha's claim to US citizenship. Without this, she was considered a citizen of Ghana, and the Lovicks would not be able to remove her from the country. Once the necessary documents were obtained, Ted Shultz flew Margaret and Marsha back to Bassari where the local Christians were eager to see the new arrival. Margaret recalls,

The African Christians from our church had to see the baby and put their hands all over her. I was afraid she would pick up germs, as babies put their hands in their mouths. So I began to pray for a carriage to take her to church. [When] Bill went to Ghana to do some shopping, I asked him to find a buggy like the English use. As soon as he arrived [back home], the buggy was the first thing he unloaded from the truck. I called it Marsha's Cadillac. I was able to cover the carriage with a net, so [people] could see her but not touch her.

In late summer of 1964, the Lovicks returned to the United States on furlough. They flew from Africa to Geneva, Switzerland, where they had a chance to visit with the friends they had made years before when they began their missions work. When they arrived in America, they were met by Bill's mother and brother and other family members. (Margaret's mother had passed away while they were on the field, and her father was a widower in Orlando, Florida.) The missionaries once again made Norfolk, Virginia, their home base while on furlough. Glad Tidings had been supporting their work faithfully over the years, and Bill had the opportunity to share with the congregation all that God had been doing in Africa.

As the holidays approached, the missionaries found their finances depleted. Their missions account had dwindled to $1.68, and there was not much hope of buying Christmas gifts that year. In mid-December, they received a call from Bill Wilkerson, a friend who owned a car dealership in Norfolk, who asked them to stop by.

When the Lovicks arrived at the dealership, Bill Wilkerson took them into his office and closed the door. He said,

I want to thank you for your letters, as they have been a blessing to me. I was having trouble at home; my wife left me and took the children. One day I told my secretary, "The first thing every morning, I will shut my door, and I do not want to be disturbed by anyone." The first hour of everyday I prayed. I said [to myself], "If God can do things for the Africans, He can surely help me." In a few weeks God restored my family to me, and I am teaching a Sunday school class.

The missionaries rejoiced with the car dealer and prayed for God's continued favor for him and his family. Before they parted, Bill Wilkerson said, "You don't have a car, so I will give you one to use while you are home. And here is a check for you for Christmas, and a set of Corning Ware."

Thinking back on that time, Margaret reflects, "Sometimes we think God has forgotten us, when we think it should come right now. Keep trusting, for He is in control of everything. Praise His holy name. By the way, that check was for $500. We had a great Christmas!"

Before the Lovicks returned to Africa, the Assemblies of God Missions Board asked them to take a new assignment in Lome, the capital city of Togo. The Wakefields, missionaries with whom the Lovicks had worked when they first arrived in Africa, had started the new work in Lome, but they had to leave the mission field and return to the States. Bill and Margaret felt led of the Lord to take the new work.

The transition to Lome required some significant changes in the couple's living conditions. Whereas in Bassari the Lovicks lived in relative comfort in a home, in Lome they lived in a camper trailer on vacant land that the Wakefields had purchased. Margaret remembers,

[The camper] had a bunk bed on each side with no mattresses. We just put quilts down to sleep on. We had a little bed [for Marsha] that we brought from the States. We put it between the beds and zippered her in so she was safe from the bugs and snakes. We were about three blocks from the Bay of Benin, back in a coconut grove. At night you could hear the wind and the waves. It was so peaceful. I loved it there.

One morning the peace was disturbed by the sounds of grunting and snorting outside the camper. Margaret lifted the flap over the screen window and peered out. She was surprised to see a mother pig and her babies meandering about the camper. She quickly called Marsha to come look. "I don't have a picture to show you what a pig looks like," Margaret told her daughter, "but God is so good; He sent a mother pig and her three little pigs to visit us."

Bill had been seeking God for direction as to where to build a church in Lome. One night, God gave him a dream of the property. He awoke full of excitement and told his wife, "God showed me the property He wants for the church! It is a street in town, and there are railroad tracks running down the center. I saw the church on that property, and it was filled with people. I'm going to find that property today."

Bill set out for the area he had seen in his dream. When he came to the place, he found the property surrounded by a tall straw mat wall. He opened the bamboo door built into the wall and stood frozen at the sight before him.

There stood the fetish god of the Ewe nation, about ten feet high with all kinds of altars around it. There were shells for its eyes, nose, mouth, and belly button. All around it lay all kinds of fetishes. There were chickens, goats, and all kinds of animals and bones covered in blood, a gruesome sight. I said, "God, You have made a mistake."

As Bill started to leave, he encountered an old man who called to him, saying, "Come white man. I want to have a talk with you." Bill eyed the man with kola nut juice dripping down the sides of his mouth and slowly walked toward him. The old man said, "I know you."

"No sir, you don't know me," Bill replied.

"You say you are the son of the most high God who lives in the heavens," the old man responded. "And last night your God gave you a dream that one day you would have a church on this piece of property. I know everything your God told you. My god told me everything your God told you, and your eyes shall never eat of what your God promised you. We will make fetish. You will die. Your wife and your child will die. You shall never eat of what [your] God has promised you."

Shaken, Bill thought, *If he meant to scare me, he did a good job of it.* He walked away from the old man, got into his jeep, and took off. When he arrived home, he told his wife, "We are going home. We are going to America. We are going on furlough today." Taken aback, Margaret asked what had happened. When Bill told her, Margaret dropped her frying pan and began dancing and speaking in tongues and glorifying God. Bill responded, "Honey, I didn't know you would be so happy about going home."

"We are not going home," Margaret replied. "We are going to build the church for the Lord Jesus Christ, and the gates of hell shall not prevail against it, today or forever." And that settled the matter. The couple determined to pursue the heavenly vision.

The missionaries contacted the owner of the property, who was not the old man Bill had encountered, and the owner agreed to sell it for $5,000. The Lovicks contacted the foreign missions department, requesting funds, but God had a different plan. The couple received a letter from a woman who said that God had spoken to her to send the missionaries $5,000 to buy a piece of property. Enclosed with the letter was a cashier's check for that exact amount. The work could go forward.

Now the property was ours, but we had a problem. How can we get the witch doctor to vacate the property?

Bill went to see the General of the Togo Army. He was escorted into his office by his body guard. The General stood up to greet him.

"Hello Pastor Lovick! I have wanted to see you for a long time. I want to thank you for bringing my brother's body to Lome. As my brother lived and died in Bassari, the family wanted him buried in the family plot in Lome. Are you still living in Basari?"

"No, I have just moved to Lome and I am going to build a church here. I have bought property, but I have a problem. It is occupied by the witch doctor and he refuses to vacate the property."

"Oh, no problem Pastor - I owe you."

He was a giant man, seven feet tall. He turned and opened his closet putting on his uniform coat that was full of metals. Calling his guard, he said, "Tell the chauffer to bring my jeep." The jeep screeched to a stop. He said, "Follow me." I followed behind, as his Jeep horn was sounding all the way there.

When we arrived, the General stepped from his Jeep. He had in his hand a long scroll. When the bugle sounded, all the people came to see what was going on. The witch doctor stepped out of his compound to see also.

He read the law to the witch doctor telling him the property belonged to the Assembly of God and he is to vacate the property in five days. I thanked him and thanked God with a sigh of relief! I thanked God we had the army working for God."

Once the property was secured and cleared, the Lovicks constructed a brush arbor and began to hold services. They used cement blocks with boards set across for seats, and since the land was prone to flooding during heavy rains, people would have to lift their feet to stay dry. For the first several weeks, attendance held steady at only three people: Bill, Margaret, and Marsha Lovick. It became so discouraging that one Sunday Margaret said to Bill, "Let's not go to church." Bill said, "No we will continue to go even if no one comes." That same morning, eight men awaited the Lovicks upon their arrival for the church service. Though Bill was learning the Ewe language, he was still not fluent in it. This particular morning, however, the Spirit of God anointed him, and he began to preach fluently in Ewe.

Through Bill, God spoke to the hearts of the eight men, who began weeping. They had come to run Bill and Margaret off, but instead, they gave their hearts to the Lord and became the first converts in the new Lome church. From that point on, the church began to grow. Eventually walls were erected, and the sanctuary was completed but not without strong opposition.

In a letter to supporters dated September 27, 1965, the Lovicks tell of the struggles they were facing in building the Lome church:

As you know, the land we purchased here in Lome was once the place dedicated to the two most powerful gods of the Ewe nation, the God of Python and the God of the Sea. God gave us the land, and the devil has been disturbed ever since and has tried every way possible to get it back.

Our native pastor was lied on and taken to jail. [Bill] was lied on and called before the Minister of Interior. Fetish was made by three people (a priest and two women) to kill [Bill]. The fetish priest was stricken by God and is completely paralyzed. [One of the women] became desperately ill and had to be hospitalized. Her treatment cost her husband about $250, which to him was his entire fortune. The second woman made public fetish against us. Someone stole her husband's new motorcycle and completely destroyed it. The husband, in turn, beat his wife terribly and said that if she had not done this bad thing against the church, God would not have allowed his cycle to be stolen. During all this we just worked and prayed as never before.

Spiritual opposition seemed to linger even after the church was under construction and dozens of people were saved. Clearly the Lovicks had hit a satanic nerve in Lome, and they had become marked people. It was no surprise, then, when Bill made plans to attend the conference in Natitingou, Dahomey, in December of 1965, that one of his associates brought a dire warning, pleading with him to cancel the trip. In the ensuing months, the Lovicks would see the Destroyer at his worst and God at His best.

Chapter Six

A sudden clap of thunder summoned Bill back to the present. Emerging through the mist of his memories, he became aware of the acute pain in his chest, and he remembered the accident. He heard the labored breathing of his wife as she lay dying in the bed next to him. He saw little Marsha lying in the bed to his other side, her leg wrapped in a cast. Thoughts of fear began to envelope him once again. He did his best to throw the care of it all on the Lord, but as one day ran into the next, his faith wavered.

For four weeks, Margaret's life hung in the balance as she lay comatose in the hospital bed. During that time, her husband hardly left her side. Near the end of that period, the doctor came into the room, listened to Margaret's heartbeat, and told Bill, "Pastor, get a casket. Your wife is not going to make it; she will not live until tomorrow." Bill walked over to the window. Outside a steady rain was falling, but inside of Bill a hurricane was swirling. He looked up to God with tears cascading down his face and cried, "God how much will You ask me to bear before I see Your hand? How much?"

He opened his eyes and saw a commotion outside of the window. Dozens of people were piling out of a large, old truck parked nearby, and racing through the rain, into the hospital. Straining his eyes, Bill recognized one, then another, and another of the Africans running toward the building. They were believers from the Lome church, and they had come to do kingdom business. Bill was astonished.

They knocked at the door and filled that room—around the bed, under the bed—and they began to bombard heaven. They had fasted for twenty-seven days. They had walked the first sixty-two miles [to the hospital] and had ridden the last few miles. They stayed on their faces before God, and they touched the King of Kings and Lord of Lords. When they got up, they said, "Pastor, we will continue as long as you need us to fast and pray." Oh for a congregation that loves their pastor like that. Oh for a congregation that loves one another like that. [A congregation] that will fast and pray until hell is given back and God is glorified. Hallelujah!

That evening, Bill was alone in the hospital room with his wife. He rested his head on Margaret's thigh and wept and prayed throughout the night. In the morning, medical personnel came in to check on Margaret's condition. She was still alive, and her breathing was stronger. They took more x-rays. By afternoon, Bill was exhausted and fell asleep. He awoke later when he felt the bed move. Opening his eyes, he saw Dr. Nkagoo removing the tubes from Margaret. Bill screamed, "No! No! My wife is not dead!" The doctor turned to Bill and said reassuringly,

Oh no pastor. We x-rayed the liver. The liver has been bleeding for thirty days, but it has fused itself off, and there is a scar where there should be a laceration. And the femur has pulled itself out of the liver. We don't understand it. What we feared would bring death has brought life. Your wife is going to live.

That same afternoon, Margaret's eyes fluttered. She opened them for a few seconds and then went back to sleep. The next morning, she awoke and said, "I am hungry." Her husband spoon fed her some broth. When the doctor returned, he listened to Margaret's heart and confirmed that it was beating normally. "She is going to make it pastor," he reiterated.

Though clearly a miracle had occurred, Margaret still had an uphill battle ahead of her. The doctors continued to pump large doses of penicillin into her body to prevent infection. Her x-rays were sent to Campbell's Clinic—a leading orthopedic surgery center in Memphis, Tennessee—for the assessment and recommendations of their physicians. Their directive was explicit: "Operate [and] remove all the bones from the right hip." Their prognosis was sobering: "She will never walk again until new advances are made in surgery."

When Bill presented this information to his wife, Margaret began to cry and laugh. Trying to console her, Bill said, "Honey, I'll take care of you. I'll love you." Margaret responded, "Bill, I am not crying about that. The twenty-nine days I lay absent from this world, I walked with Him who is King of Kings and Lord of Lords. I shall walk again for the glory of almighty God. I shall walk again. I know I shall."

When Margaret was finally released from the hospital, she was still in a great deal of pain. The Lovicks spent several days with Wayne Turner and his family in Cotonou before returning to Lome. While at the Turners, Bill remembers watching his wife struggle to get out of bed:

I could not help her, for it would hurt her. I would hear her get off the bed on her left knee, and she would be weeping and praying, telling God, "I've given You everything, this life, this body, this soul; it's all Yours Lord. You promised to heal me. When Lord? When Lord?"

As if the pain from the accident was not enough, Margaret was bitten on the toe by a rat while sleeping. The rat had come in through a hole in the roof of the Turner's residence and found its way under Margaret's sheets. A doctor gave her a tetanus shot for the bite and told Bill they could resume traveling in a few days.

On April 13, 1966, nearly four months after Margaret first entered the hospital, she returned to the mission station in Lome. Her right leg was almost four inches shorter than her left leg, and she continued to receive large doses of penicillin daily. On her first Sunday back, Margaret said to her husband, "Put me on the cot and take me to church. I want to see my children. I want to see my women." Bill remembered,

I heard her scream sometime whenever she moved, but I carried her to church, and she taught her children; she taught her women. No wonder her classes grew, because of the price she dared pay for the glory of God. I remember when we first started the church in Lome, and we were under the brush arbor, she would pray, "God, send us revival at any cost." That is a serious prayer, and here it was happening. What a price. But it could not compare to what Jesus paid for our souls.

With each passing day, Margaret showed signs of improving. Bill announced that he was organizing a city-wide revival for the following month, and the news energized his wife. She coordinated the stuffing of fifteen thousand envelopes with promotional material for the campaign, setting twenty-five envelopes aside in faith.

"What are they for?" Bill asked.

"The day that revival starts, I'll walk down the street by the grace and power of God, and I'll give them out," Margaret affirmed.

The following day, Bill was fixing the roof on the church and praying for his wife as he worked. He heard the still, small voice of the Holy Spirit say, "Go home," so he immediately climbed down from the roof and hurried home. But he soon realized that God had arrived before him.

"I felt like I was on holy ground," Bill recalled as He tried to describe the presence of God that he felt in his home. He remembered his wife explaining how God had come into her room, taken her by the leg, and pulled it. She had felt a tearing sensation and screamed with pain, "Bones come into place!" Bill turned the covers back to check Margaret's leg. It was four inches longer than it had been. He put some pressure on it, and it held.

Later that same day, Margaret took her husband by the arm and walked the streets, distributing twenty-five packets of Gospel literature to the glory of God. On the third night of the crusade, she walked unassisted up onto a six-foot high platform in front of an audience of thousands. Seeing and sharing her triumph, the multitude rose to their feet and shouted praises to the living God.

When the church building was near completion, the Lovicks invited missionary-evangelists Paul Olson Jr., his father, and Harris Heinrich for the outdoor crusade. A colonel from the Togo army flew Bill in a plane over the city, dropping leaflets that announced the meetings. The excitement spread even to the marketplace as people marched around the vendor's stalls singing the hymn "Marching with the King." Africans responded to the Gospel message with a surprising eagerness. In just over three weeks, 4,375 people accepted the Lord in the open-air crusade. Many of these new converts also were healed and filled with the Holy Spirit during two weeks of follow-up meetings held in the new church building. For the first time in Lome's history, its residents experienced a Pentecostal outpouring like that found in the Book of Acts.

On Sunday, February 25, 1968, after years of struggle, the new church building, named Calvary Temple, was officially dedicated. It was a joyous occasion that was attended by political and religious dignitaries. Colonel Kleber Dadjo, Minister of Justice for Togo, cut the ribbon to begin the ceremonies. Also attending was the US Ambassador to Togo Albert W. Scherer, Jr. and his wife Carroll; R. Stanley Berg, a minister from New York City and guest speaker for the event; Ralph Wilkerson, who would later pastor Melodyland Christian Center in Anaheim, California; and Don Wilkerson of Teen Challenge in Brooklyn, New York. One of the highlights of the event was the unveiling of the distinctive hand carved wooden sanctuary doors, which depicted scenes from the life of Christ.

The celebration climaxed two days later with an official reception hosted by Ambassador and Mrs. Scherer at the US Embassy. Bill recalled, "We had prayed God would send us a revival at any cost. Sometimes God calls us to pay a higher price than we expected. [...] He sent us a wonderful revival. I'm sure the angels in heaven were rejoicing with us at the dedication of Calvary Temple."

The year 1969 brought further change into the Lovick family with the adoption of a baby boy, whom they named William David Lovick. Like Marsha, David cut his teeth on the mission field. Shortly after adopting their son, the Lovick family received a new commission to go to Zaire (known today as the Democratic Republic of the Congo), located in Central Africa. David adapted remarkably well to the life of a missionary. And after finishing his schooling in America several years later, he returned to Zaire to assist his father. He was in the capital city of Kinshasa with Bill one day in the mid 1990s when tragedy struck.

Bill was standing in the yard outside his home, trying to get reception on his new mobile phone, when he suddenly dropped the phone and collapsed. He had suffered a seizure. David rushed to aid his father and had him flown to a hospital in South Africa. The doctors who attended Bill gave him the grim news that he had a brain tumor and leukemia. Bill returned to the US, and under the care of doctors and by the grace of God, he was able to postpone death for a few years. Before he left Africa, however, he told the African pastors that he would return.

Eventually Bill developed another tumor in his chest that spread to his brain, and he knew his time was short. In March of 1996, two months before his death, he said, "I am going back to Africa to put things in order." Accompanied by his doctor and two minister friends, he returned to Zaire and bid his African pastors farewell. On May 16, 1996, Bill Lovick breathed his last breath and measured off a life wholly dedicated to serving the Everlasting God. Today the work in Africa continues from the seeds that Bill and Margaret Lovick so lovingly sewed for over forty years. To God be the glory.

CPSIA information can be obtained
at www.ICGtesting.com
Printed in the USA
FFHW021027031218
49720460-54137FF